Monotheism and Pathology

I0095796

Established April 2023

New York, NY

United States of America

ISBN: 978-1-971928-06-7

Monotheism and Pathology

Psychology meets Philosophy

Baruch Menache

Author's Notation:

This work is an intersection of psychology and philosophy, with the subject of psychology as the criteria of research. The reference of Egyptian dynasties is a mere illustration of an ancient culture. As well, the reference of monotheism is to apportion what would be considered a contemporary manifestation — if retrogressively interjected back into history, moreover, this is not to be confused with the everyday usage of the word or concept, e.g., religions. The idea would be the deactivation of the word and concept when all things considered, but as of yet, is still the area of research that requires this retrogressive mode of research. This is the susceptibility of *retrogressive research* and should be remembered throughout this work. The objective is to emphasize contemporary concepts within the field of psychology rather than validate precedents of history.

Table of Contents

Monotheism 39

Monotheism and Civilization 59

Consciousness 71

Pathology is Natural 79

Pathology: The Definition

Encountering the psychological tradition had my research extend to the realization that the concept of pathology is rudimentary to higher life form consciousness. In psychoanalysis, we absorb the notion that all mental complications can be attributed to an incoherent internal dialogue. When we perceive the psyche's function and model it upon the biological system, it has the characteristic of losing functionality when its components are not appropriately interacting. Thus, dictating to us that the interaction of the psyche's contents is the basis for a functioning psyche; and consequently, proper sociality.

We could stipulate that psychological research was inherited from an intuitive awareness of this concept, accepting the principle that there is such a structure as a functional psyche. This functionality interacts interactively and roots an absolute psyche. When nearer to that functionality, it secures the absolute procedure of the psyche, and while distant, to be improperly using the apparatus.

This theory becomes evident when we observe how the specialist seeks to analyze the substructure of internal dialogue, uncovering what remains hidden in the internal conversation, particularly the subconscious. Through the process of being in quest of certain content which has been neglected, overlooked, or repressed, we bring the patient to a *former* state in which the system of the psyche *was* more integrated and functional. Under this perspective, the awareness of the subconscious would not be perceived as novel components—compelled to ascend from the unknown; rather, should be viewed as material which did not receive the overarching attention that it thoroughly deserved. The platform of the psyche should have regaled more activity for that particular content. The notion that it ought to manifest only as there is a functional sub-layer in which the psyche is subservient; thereby demanding a certain direction of integration. The subconscious should have been integrated, which leads to the thesis that integration is the form of a high-functioning psyche and disintegration; a low-functioning.

The Arbitrator of Thoughts

Therefore, we will be using that aspect of disintegration in terms of one of its psychological names; pathology. The basis of pathology, when viewed as an active force and not merely as a process of thinking, attempts to undermine the universality of thought. This sanctions to an over-or-under-stimulation of certain thoughts, even as they warrant proper consideration. That degree of attention-demand is based on the amount of relevance contained by the entire substructure. For example, the designer of a project would devote limited resources to the less relevant sections and would rather balance the expenditure in a fashion that would be distributed according to the attention-demand of each component of the project. We could formulate that each portion of the project has a percentage of attention-demand which is consequent of the overall project and will be apportioned accordingly.

Although the intrinsic sectors do not mandate any attention with reference to themselves, and is indeed voiced from an enacted identity as being a part of the project. The *project* is the agent that diversifies the resources according to the needs of the project. To determine the amount that something warrants, one must articulate an arbitrator to oversee the situation. The objective arbitrator is necessary because there is an unavailability of either the sector or the project as being capable to self-reflect in consequence to what is beyond their individualized nature. The sector does not comprehend its position in the scheme of things and the project doesn't achieve the sentience of various components; being in the elevated position external to the sector. The individuation within the internality of the project will not be allowed to recognize those general needs, and only with a certain disjointed oversight will be tasked with such a thing.

The Unsuccessful Arbitrator

When we confer that patterns of thought are *deserving* attention, we rely on an overarching arbitrator to assign value to each thought. In effect, we are defining the basic structure for which pathology: *in its neglect to account for this arbitrator, or its perception in a misguided manner*. Pathology is not a form by itself, just as dysfunctionality is not a positive form of existence; they rather rely on another concept, when neglected, gives rise to its significance.

Moreover, neglecting the arbitrator who is tasked with the oversight of thought is the primary factor to contribute to pathological thinking. Second to neglect, is a wrongful perception of the arbitrator, taking the assumed role of a particular commander all the while deferential to another. The arbitrator is a fluid construct, its build is based on the present moment, to which we cannot produce an objective to counter as a greater form of arbitration. The method to determine the degree of arbitration is in reference to the universal psyche system and the particular content's relevancy, much like the project which determines particular sectors to be justified with more consideration.

To illustrate the difference between neglecting the arbitrator and fabricating the entity with presuppositions, as neglecting entails the deprivation of a formulated psyche hierarchy, in which a single component remains more authoritative than all other thoughts. Only when prohibiting interactive components to be granted its crucial stations, will it consent to the negation of an arbitration. By setting aside certain interactive elements to remain dominant, one will become available to perform arbitration for the rest of the psyche. For instance, setting a moment in memory to be interactive, will give access to determine the remainder of the psyche in relation to that. However, when one does not find any interactive aspect to be worthwhile of extra attention, it will not offer the ability for a ruling class to relate to the distributing components of the psyche, becoming a conglomerate of short-lived animations.

The second form of corruption occurs when one perceives the arbitrator to be all-encompassing, placing existential safety and dread upon it. They dictate the power-rights of assigning an arbitrator to be aligned with that particular fixation. This creates a wrongful perception of the arbitrator, which is not the sum of the psyche's contents, being restricted to limited parameters. To be precise, the existential projection is the universality of existence, which is determined to be found and dealt with in this singular aspect. The existential dread which we are all privy, is among other things, a manifestation of all the known and unknown aspects of personhood, to which we are now applying to a known aspect; an illogicality to place what is intrinsically unknown to a known criterion.

When one weighs these forms of corruption, whether from neglecting the wholesome arbitrator or a wrongful perception, it allows for unrestricted and natural movement for all pathways of thought; the resultant of a diminishment in pathological thinking. However, the failure to perceive this arbitrator in a proper manner can also affect the final production of thought. For example, if an individual exaggerates another social being, thus incorporating their persona within their identity, it will sanction an embodied narrative to have a share in that arbitrator. This might be done, and usually is, without conscious acknowledgment. Because of the fact that they are modeled as a diversion to avoid major vulnerabilities, and might we say the entire vulnerability apparatus, it would constitute a sensitive topic for subjective selfhood. When thoughts arise contrary to how this assumed persona represents itself, it will not be certified its proper attention and due course. That exaggerated sentiment will assume the role of arbitrator in as much as thoughts are contrary to its agenda.

To annotate: on no account is it characteristically pathological to glorify aspects or beings, as there remains objective material that may be available and can only arrive through such identification. The pathological aspect comes into play when the identification takes the role of arbitrator and primacy of thought, as there is little to no interaction with the identification and rather is the presumed position of existence. We will discuss the need for certain pathology that assists in productive expansion, for there is a version that has one pathologically proclaim against pathology.

Another occasion for a wrongful perception of an arbitrator is when an individual perceives themselves in an insufficient manner within the social landscape. Their sufficiency is relied on by the perceived universal reality to which the social community represents. A lone individual is organically sufficient in their respective biological state; however, this sufficiency is not presumed to be the universal reality. The individual does not accept their biological sufficiency because they acknowledge a realistic framework to which they partake but are not alone in. It doesn't help that we can easily construct a conception that a biological system relies on the social community for sustenance and reproduction.

This is a sleight of hand, for it wasn't the dependency of the social environment which assumed personhood to be lacking sufficiency, but rather within personhood expanse and its biological sufficiency, one recognizes a superior level of resources in the social realm. The center of sufficiency is still the organism; however, the external reality is holding a surplus of possibility for organic attainment. A tree bearing fruit would be considered a possibility for the organism but not to be attributed as the sufficiency of the organism. There is a token of truth, to which the resources are a partiality of one's sufficiency, utilizing a concept of sufficiency that is individualized for the application of a universal realm.

Although the social community contains resources, an individual chooses where and when to allocate them. That specific process is self-sufficient, while the social community is a secondary sufficiency. The communal sentiment creates a sufficiency proclamation that is in reference to the universal framework, while insufficiency is manufactured from our attachment to it. Residing in the wild will not have one partake in a system that extends beyond oneself, as a result, would not recognize a complex sufficiency structure. This perception of insufficiency will conscript as an arbitrator of thoughts and will not permit contrary thoughts to manifest themselves on the platform of the psyche. We may want to venture and state that all principles—ideas which are beyond logic, take the same role for the psyche. This, of course, depends on the integration of principles within the identity of the person.

The Contrast of Internal vs. External Experience

We must be prompt at this interval that in evolutionary terms, external experience cannot replace internal experience. Something separate from selfhood cannot integrate within selfhood, let alone take over as a chief arbitrator of thought processes. This, as we will elaborate in a further context, is only possible through the role of identity. When one identifies with someone or something, in accordance with the biological system the identification is a part of the system. The principle, whatever it may be, will take over as arbitrator, only according to the degree of identification with that principle. When there is a threat against one's identity, it is experienced as a threat against the organic self, even as the threat is not seeking to undermine one's existence.

The principle is only possible thanks to the ability of identification which causes one to be integral to that principle. This allows ideas that are not systematically reasonable, to be reasonable enough, and thus to be a part of personhood through identity. This is because anything that is integrated within selfhood does not require reasonability to be considered a form of existence. *The state of selfhood runs indifferent to the coherence of itself, and one may never obtain complete reasonability for one's intrinsic existence.* Existence does not necessitate a justification of itself, it simply exists as a natural state of expression. Rationality and justification are tools that are used upon the state of existence, which as we have stated is not innately rational.

We will always find individuals who have made use of the outfit of rationality and coherency to question their innate existence; they will be using these tools to undermine the basis which allows these tools to be expressed. That being the case, whatever is to be considered a part of selfhood will enjoy the liberty of not necessitating meaning or logic. "We are who we are," "it is, what it is," and other related notions which pertain to the privation of prerequisite for reasonability in intrinsic components of selfhood.

Existence and Reasonability

We may desire to apply this viewpoint for all existence, utilizing such stipulations to uproot the need for reasonability; hence the axiom, "it is, what it is" can be relevant for any area, idea, or experience. We would necessitate a philosophy for tolerating this perspective, to require a quantity of logic and reason, but once the sentiment is integrated into commonality it loses that prerequisite. The grounds for not necessitating a theory to the already applied sentiment, is that selfhood is a motorized autonomy which doesn't concern its reasons for existence. A higher-life-form, intrinsically does not care about its innate nature. In the contemporary era, we have gained strides in the realm of rationality and consciousness, granting the amenity to be critical about an array of subjects. This, being considered an amenity, is of extreme importance, a non-essentiality of an individual, manifesting during periods of tranquility and progression.

This feat of progression does not fade the simplistic base layer of higher life forms. The main realm of reasonability is for external stimuli, which is the threatening other, assisting us to select our integration or lack thereof. Selfhood is like a superintendent that is the source of all quandaries and cannot be questioned, whereas, what is external to selfhood would be considered the mortal reality, in which one must adhere to exacting rules of nature. We can invert the clause and use critical thinking in contradiction of selfhood, constituting an existential crisis. With a limited extension, this may be the correct course of inquiry but as we have stated, does not necessitate inquiry at all.

The Use for Rationality

When the contents of the psyche are considered members of existence, we may question the need for rationality. The psyche, just as in all existence, should be allowed the advantage of freedom from coherence and logic. Thoughts should be certified in their flow, in whatever manner they happen to stream, all according to their biological connections. Theoretically, this notion is valid, yet higher-life-forms have extended consciousness to a degree that allocates and apportions the manipulation of the psyche in any direction. With this regulation over the apparatus, it no longer has its natural biological process as a protective mechanism and rather comprises a higher-life-form footprint on its mechanisms. Therefore, by taking charge of the system, differing from mammals, they must account for coherency in how they manage this complex system. This is different from the manner of existence itself, in which higher life forms have not had any interaction to permit existence to be. Existence remains outside the realm of control and integration, as a substructure beneath active consciousness, which does not adhere to the laws of justice, coherency, or logic.

When higher life forms reach a state to which existence is a realm that they can manipulate, such discussions may be necessary. The mammal which does not have the facility to actively control the sequence of thoughts does not need the remedy of rationality or logic. When a mammal seems to be engaging in irrationality, we can attribute the condition to a biological mishap which disrupts the psyche process. Higher life forms, when engaging in irrationality are to be measured as executing those mistakes; such will be the view as long as there is a justice system.

Principles to Permit Irrationality

An individual who believes their individuality to be in a certain supposition will be entering a realm of irrationality that automatically effectuates an identity. One cannot inherently participate in an irrational thought process since the expected biological process manifests in a rational manner; for even a mammal will be assumed to abide by a rational system. The manner in which a higher life form will be able to engage in irrationality otherwise known as pathology, is through the device of identity. In management of the system, by adding external components, all to be perceived as internal, the psyche will be able to hedge into any arena without the consequence of negating its biological function.

As such, the attachment to an identity is experienced in fluctuating degrees; the determinant degree is one which has the identity becoming the command as arbitrator of thought patterns. A large portion of thought patterns must pass through the checkpoint of this supposition, which facilitates as a filter for incoming thoughts. The filter is tasked to mark each thought with either of three labels; unrelated to the supposition or identity, enhancing the point at hand, or contrary to the identity or supposition. In *Nineteen Eighty-Four*, the general thesis of its governing body for impending information was such; to assist the current agenda, to damage it, or to be deemed irrelevant.[1]

For illustration, if one is in a social culture that admonishes certain sexual behavior, becoming a part of one's identity will constitute a filter with a reference to the process of one's thinking. When sexual thoughts arise, especially those that go contrary to cultural normativity, one will not tolerate its expression to manifest in normal function. While if they arise to affirm the cultural norm, they will be highlighted and encouraged with superfluous exuberance. The identity serves as an arbitrator of the psyche and sits behind the sequence of thoughts to ensure that it meets certain requirements.

Since the persona at large is part in parcel with the supposition, anything contrary to its thesis becomes a threat to the persona and thus existence. Therefore, this principle is permitted into the private sector of arbitrators, to adopt the entire flow of the psyche. From this vantage point, all thoughts will pass through this censorship with the objective of diminishing the contrarian arguments while highlighting those that follow its thesis. Just as if a biological

---

[1] Orwell, G., *Nineteen Eighty-Four*, 1949.

addition was grafted to the organic system, these primary thoughts and principles are considered beyond mental connections, to become flesh and bone. This gives cognitive justification for such an imposition, being that one is protecting a biological additive, to which the psyche's function is always subservient.

Right and Wrong Thoughts

When we study pathology, we will inevitably result in a distinction between correct and incorrect forms of thinking. Even as we would like to avoid making such political demands, in that we would be associating thoughts to be *wrong* or *right*, this remains an integral part of the study of pathology. This moral judgment results from the meta-analysis of thought, not so much the content of thoughts but its relation to other thoughts. Similarly, we would dictate that ingesting food into one's body is the right thing to do, even as there may be points of conjecture when taking reason towards certain patterns of thought such as the philosophy of an anorexic. Existence which will function at its optimal level is the basis of our contextual morality.

Thoughts like any other form of biology do not arise in a vacuum, being that it contains its authority through neighboring thoughts. The *right* thought would arise through a natural fluidity between its neighboring thoughts. The thought is not driven forward in a manner that would appear from nowhere, nor does it diminish into the abyss; despite the pressing demand for change from the surrounding environment. There is a hierarchy to the potency of certain thoughts, especially those that relate to one's intrinsic existence and this concept will be appreciated by neighboring thoughts. According to the standard of all thoughts, it is agreed that a certain designation for a certain thought is a justified attribution. When the standard of thoughts or all the possible neighboring thoughts do not democratically agree to that attribution, it would be a manifestation of pathological thinking.

For instance, if a sequence of thoughts that are related to a trauma induced pattern of thought are in agreement to allow such thoughts to be neurotically repeated. The memory is sanctified, and all other thoughts will adjust accordingly. Yet, a memory of a trauma may be broadened more than the standard agreement of its potency, in which the highly esteemed thought is being recognized notwithstanding of its neighbors. One may pity themselves, by doing so, would be taking upon themselves the identity of a pathetic person. This subsequently develops a filter that aggrandizes the trauma of maintaining that particular identity.

Psyche components may worry about a repeat experience of the traumatic event and will aggrandize the trauma to ensure that it does not get repeated.

However, the apprehension itself is also a thought that is subservient to a degree of standard attention. When the fear accounts for more attention than the neighboring thoughts would permit, it becomes pathological. Courage would be an allowance for other thoughts, than those of worry, to be allowed articulation despite the emotional demand that existential dread presumes.

To summarize, the psyche naturally coalesces to a coherently functional state and this is despite the emotional responses of each particular thought. Surely, the psyche accounts for the weightily tangled thoughts and is in deference to its influence. When thoughts pertain to a threat of the organism, the psyche will adhere to those thoughts with acute focus and deliberation. No neighboring thought will seek to interfere as it is understood that it is pertinent to the entire biological system. The emotional allocation to a particular thought is to what degree it attaches to the existential components of personhood.

The Paradox of Pathology

Even though the study of pathology is only about the relation of thoughts with each other, and surely not an appraisal of the content of thoughts, still, we must conceptualize those relations; meaning the mechanisms in conjunction with tangible concepts. Pathology can be the mechanism that prevents concepts or conceptualizations from interchanging with other thought material. We may call this 'hypocrisy' or a 'double standard', alluding to portions of the psyche which are not consistent with other portions; in the case of the double standard, it's the portion that is related to certain behaviors or activity. One may engage in a concept or idea in a specific situation while neglecting to recollect its substance in the intervention of another. What we are accenting is not the individual's paradoxical nature, which can be said for all inquiries, but only the neglect of integration or dialogue between two standards.

We are bound to the paradox and cannot expect a singular understanding, for instance in the romantic field, to partake equivalently with all relationships. What is known in a peculiar state of stupor, and the behavior that it prompts, will become disremembered in a non-overestimated relational activity. Our level of awareness by no means will thoroughly permeate every aspect.

A mathematician will certainly not reach a state in which every other component of the psyche is integrated with a mathematical layer. Even if it were the case, the external discipline of mathematics will always supersede mathematical comprehensions in other aspects. The study of psychology is soberly apparent in this regard, in which the knowledge obtained in the study will not be equally integrated into all aspects of the psyche, notwithstanding being the research of the psyche. One will not be able to apply the material to personal relationships or disciplines in the same manner that the study itself conveys.

Hitherto that we must deal with these paradoxes, we understand that neglecting to have broader considerations to influence particular aspects would be pathological territory. The active neglect of sanctioning a comprehension of a single discipline to impinge on another is pathology. The inactive neglect, in which one has never considered the discipline in certain arenas, would be an unassuming neglect and not considered for pathology. There is no mechanism within the psyche that has halted that integration of thought; attributed to the notion of not being forecasted.

Pathology does not bother with the paradox, as it is a part of the natural biological function. By being a multiplicity, we are always within the realm of participation in one arena to contrast another; the paradox remains. Pathology only pertains to the conscious neglect or over-stimulation of thoughts. It's as if a third-party mechanism which is demanding the paradox be fulfilled, regardless of the clear value for rebalancing the system.

The Link between Pathology and Monotheism

Pathology is either the fixating emphasis or the fixating neglect of certain patterns of thought. The subjective experience of pathological thinking would be identified when finding oneself wedged within the psyche; an absence of mental flow. Our thesis is to bridge psychology with the ancient notion of Theos, or the theory of a categorical Theos. This joining, even if established, should not be robust or to remain consistently connected, since each discipline, the one of monotheism and the one of psychology, should remain esteemed in its singularity, in which they will prosper at best.

Psychology is the discipline that becomes an advantage for being afflicted with mental dysfunction and should be the leading discipline for that regard. Monotheism and its theological equivalents have become the domain of religion and are advantageous in the realm of existential consideration and collective identity. When monotheism and its subsidiaries begin to reconcile with mental dysfunction, both the theory and the patient undergo an unjust science. When psychology attempts to violate existential issues, especially collective identities, it becomes fairly incoherent and cult-like. Allowing a new science to define traditional identities causes tradition to fade and has the science appear to lack nuance and subtlety.

Moreso, the religious offshoot of monotheism deals with existential inquiry, a topic that does not require complete rationality, while the healing process necessitates to be operated with complete rationality. As we have stated, when dealing with the question of existence, it does not require the usage of complete rationality, since rationality is a *tool of existence*. Therefore, religion is a study concerning existence and is allowed the expansive territory of rationality, irrationality, and imagination. Religion is also a collective identity, which as an identity, becomes incorporated with the biological substructure of a social being. The association with a religion does not have to be explained in rationalizing terms as it becomes existence itself; a predecessor to rationality. When religion departs the confines of existential inquiry it becomes quite wearisome, encroaching a domain where exclusive rationality can reside. We find that psychology detests the irrational approach, being science-based, while not being of ample assistance for the exploration of existential aspects for it requires commitment and imagination.

However, there is an argument that religion is a manifestation of monotheism; a supposition that is befittingly a rational science-based theory. We would never want to approach existential inquiry, for instance, religion, without a complete rational theory of the workings of the inner systems. Analogous to a child who has had an educational deficiency, to then begin the examination of existential queries, so that the tools, being the theoretical framework are being utilized for the system itself. We must make use of our systems to inquire about the existence of those systems, moreover, when those systems are underdeveloped, the resulting inquiry will be the same. We would need an educated theory to understand our system, prior to making use of it for existential inquiry. Religious identity and its existential queries are manifestations of that theory.

The monotheistic notion of a categorical Theos is a scientific theory. This should not be confused with religion or theology, which as we have stated concerns itself with existential questions. For this inquiry, monotheism is to be perceived by the psychological experience of those who adhered to its credence. Monotheism is a tool that the psychological psyche has been using and is worthy of a *psychological study*. The manifestation of a categorical Theos and its religions which have sprouted from that, although also a psychological experience, are more related to identity and other such concepts. Importantly, we would not want to use the psychological inquiry to surmise religion and theology, as the study of any discipline deserves the foremost right to surmise itself.

Monotheism and Religion

If we were to study the psychological aspect of identity and would make use of religion in that regard, we still would not be explaining religion, only the psychological manifestation of identity. When we are seeking out the concept of monotheism, we are not defining for the purpose of theology. As monotheism stands in terms of the discipline of theology, it relates both to psychological concepts and non-psychological aspects, so we are not accurately covering the discipline of theology. *The task is to understand pathology in the example of monotheism, not monotheism in the example of pathology.* For a case in point, the principle of a categorical Theos asserts an interconnectedness with all of nature, while the psychological manifestation only considers the interconnectedness of the psyche. The principle in a categorical Theos asserts that higher life forms are part of a cosmic universality, while psychology doesn't dare inquire into the value which higher life forms play in the cosmic arena. We don't want to integrate two dissimilar disciplines for the sake of simplicity, thereby causing many components of study to be lost from each.

The reason we would even want to find the notion of pathology in monotheism is because there is a certain scientific introduction that monotheism played for the primordial realm. When we postulate that rationality and coherency are the results of the monotheistic notion, we are stipulating that monotheism is scientific. It does encroach upon existential studies, being that it is a theory on all phenomena, including existential phenomena. Yet, being that monotheism becomes apportioned into existential and non-existential aspects, it gets coupled together. However, before the historical precedent approached the existential questions that amplified major religions, it was a notion that was concerned about the physical universe and not metaphysical aspects. The metaphysical aspects would no doubt become included; all experience is under the same classification, although that premise is a consequence of monotheism and not its core thesis.

If we were to postulate that monotheism and associated religions were a theological discipline from the onset, there would be no reason to connect two distinct disciplines. This is based on the assumption that religious identity and its ritualistic association is a fractional aspect of monotheism. This would have us explore the depth and breadth of these religious institutions to produce the entire monotheistic picture. But thankfully, this is not the case, since religious identity is only an outcome and derivative of monotheism. There is a scientific aspect to the monotheistic notion, which is the basis of its proposition, and to revisit that notion by recognizing the comparisons to pathology is a worthy cause.

Fundamentally, monotheism does not concern itself with the idiosyncrasies of daily life or even communal life. It is something which transcends everyday activities and cannot be reduced to religious identities. The basis of its proposition; every aspect of phenomena and experience is interconnected. Therefore, the religious identity, being separate from the mainframe of individual experience becomes contrary to its proposition. The reason that it will most likely result alongside monotheism is that the interconnected proposition has a clause which demands all of these secondary derivatives.

Monotheism's Clause

The clause is such that even as everything is interconnected, certain connections are more interactive. For example, the connection to one's innate body is of a more interactive nature, meaning that there are more connections within itself than shrubbery of the wild. The foliage is interwoven into our experience but not relative to the same extent that it is to our organic structure, so that the attention towards our system would be in proportion to the interactive environment of that connection. Therefore, we must view the interconnection of monotheism as bound to a center which, as it spreads away from the center, has fewer interactive properties than what is most near to its epicenter.

Therefore, there are two aspects to define monotheism: interconnection and the level of interaction within each specific interconnection. In truth, from an objective point of view, it is only singular, interconnectedness; however, the interactive potency must be recognized when dialogical. This energy is a natural manifestation of nature and should not be noted as anything significant, naturally attending to the superior interactive connections than its lesser counterparts. The attention itself is natural to all of nature with equal interconnectedness, yet some of nature is more interconnected than others.

For example, a doctor would naturally take note of the more significant components of the organic body, not for the fact that they have a proclivity towards the extremities. This is done as a natural response to the fact that the extremities comprise a more interconnected potency than the non-extremities. The brain entertains has interconnected properties that far exceed a limb and therefore will be viewed as a sub-body of its identifiable posture. Comparable in how we decide to study phenomena in proportion to the amount of knowledge they may contain. There is no inherent bias to this approach; we are attending to phenomena in relation to its interactive properties. Therefore, monotheism is comprehensive universality even though there will be elements within the universal landscape that deserve more attention than other elements.

This leads us to the religious identity, a service to the necessary attention of the more interactive properties of experience. This is to fulfill the absolute monotheistic notion, which includes all of universality alongside the proper attention to all its more universal components. *Religious identity is the universality of the components of universality.* This brands religious identity as a subsidiary to the monotheistic notion, to be only in complete service to it. We can imagine monotheism without religious identity, yet as time goes along, the universality of the components will not be addressed adequately. One who is conscientious of such, even without religious identity will be able to maintain a true monotheistic perspective with various tools.

Monotheism is a scientific notation for it is making a claim on reality and will never seek to depart from the perceived reality of the era. The only aspect that may be lost to the scientific purview is that it does not seek to maintain complete evidence of its identifiable notion. As it is postulating universality, it continually seeks to transcend the perceived reality by being a posture of what is universal. Monotheism never wants to be pinpointed within nature, for then it will not be a form of true universality but only a representation for such. Therefore, even as it is a theory, when we find ease in knowing its basis, we start to detach from the rubric of its postulation.

The Vulnerability of Monotheism

Thereby, we are arriving at another aspect in understanding monotheism; it transcends the notion that it postulates for itself. Monotheism is a theory of universality and comprises components that have a unique universality for dealing with their respective correspondence. Monotheism is a theory which regales in the unknown aspect, all the while being a theory concerning reality as known to individuals. This inconsistency is understandable when we become aware of the fissures in self-derived awareness. We know that there are things that we don't know, even though we cannot acknowledge that to be completely true. The knowledge of knowing that we don't know is not a true notion. We are relying on historical confirmation, but we can never know that we don't know as a consequence of not knowing. Therefore, monotheism is the theory of universality for what we know, although it transcends universality by the notion that we know that we don't know. Whenever we postulate a proposition about all of reality, it must take into account the higher life form attribute of knowing that they don't know.

Secondly, we must account for the distribution of the proposition through all the levels of locality, which would have its notion copy itself throughout its distribution. For example, a sovereign would not be able to unremittingly participate in all instructions but would have individuals copy those ideas, which could then be distributed to the lowest echelons of the populace. The result is that the populace embodies the sovereign's persona, even with the precedent of being contrary to the direct command, "this is not what they truly meant." The proposition of monotheism must be distributed so that each component would entertain its definite interconnectedness bubble. The bubble would have its own "universe", correspondingly to the religious identity being a "universal" system, in that the distribution of monotheism must be scalable.

The Rationality of Monotheism

Now that we can depart from religious identity without affecting the monotheistic notion, we can divert our attention to a dilemma within the domain of monotheism. We have stated that there is a situated universality at each level of nature, as the interactive potency of certain parts are higher than others. There must be an epicenter which encompasses the furthermost interactive elements, as to the heart is to the individual. This epicenter could be viewed from two angles, individualistic or naturalistic.

The individualistic perspective is such that we are only engaging the notion of monotheism from an individual perspective, thereby the epicenter is subjectively bound to our thoughts, and the interactive potency is only relative to ourselves.

The naturalistic approach would stipulate that there is an expected epicenter amongst nature that contains the highest levels of interactive potency, for which the higher life form is nearer to that epicenter than the excesses of known nature. Higher life forms are not the epicenter itself, but rather are adjacent, while the true epicenter is yet to be known.

The mammal's perspective would signify their distance from the epicenter of interactive potency, but then again, enough to recognize higher life forms to be such an entity. The mammal would be at variance in having to attend to their inborn epicenter, as their subjective developments are relevant to selfhood; indeed, they are compelled to recognize that higher life forms are an approximation of the epicenter. The question is as follows, in the naturalistic approach, why would the mammalian entity find its selfhood to be most relevant even as nature fails to corroborate them as being adjacent to the potent interactive center? This may compel us to recognize the other approach, which assumes the individual, by any definition, to be the epicenter; merely for the fact that we are discussing this from a subjective conjecture. While the mammal will be equivalent to human form in its experience of their innate nature, subjectively presuming itself to be at the epicenter of the universe. They would view higher life forms as another nonsignificant element of nature.

We can understand the dilemma by attending to the less complex elements of nature, for instance, a tree. The tree's perspective would not account for its interactive potency with the same stamina as would a mammal. The mammal would protest with great stamina at the notion of severing its epicenter, or existence, while the tree seems to remain reserved. This phenomenon can be presumed as a disinterest of selfhood, without approximating the naturalistic epicenter, granting a minor interest for it to flourish. The mammal can be seen contesting for survival as not a prearranged system for protecting itself, and rather validating the notion of their epicenter as an interactive force within nature.

If we follow the chain of mammalians, we find that their relationship to selfhood is not organized by their organic structure, one of mere survival. We find that they reference their selfhood in the recognition of their proximity to epicentral potency; inherent in nature and not in themselves. They are presenting stamina for survival because the proximity of that epicenter is nearby and should be acknowledged for its relevance in the universal system. This is not for its inborn objectives but for the objective of the epicenter that transcends their innate organism. This culminates in higher life forms who do not find themselves to be interactively potent only on account of self-service. They are enacting the true nature of their existence as being adjacent to an interactive potency for which they are seeking to protect; an epicenter of interaction that happens to be at stake in their intrinsic beings.

This theory would, in consequence, denounce higher life forms' assumption that they are at the absolute point of the epicenter, but rather approximate it. There is something else that is more interactive, more potent than higher life forms, and will seek to protect itself with more stamina than higher life forms. Therefore, the highest potency of interaction is also the strongest component of the universal system. The religious identity seeks to recognize the most potent interactive element in which a higher life form takes the role of a serious proponent, being adjacent to the epicenter.

Religious Identity and the Epicenter

Nonetheless, religious identity is also concerned with the true epicenter that lies beneath higher life forms, one which is more interactive and deserving of recognition in the universal system. This would be the named Theos in any religious tradition, which has the attributes of being more interactive than higher life forms. They are incorporating the epicenter notion among the elements of those that are in close proximity to it. Since the true epicenter is not known to higher life forms, it would be troublesome to postulate its specificities as it may be a deviation from the universal system. At best, the epicenter is recognized as a more interactive being, which has similar attributes to the higher life form adjacent to it. Indeed, the manner in which higher life forms are the epicenter in reference to animals is how this being is the epicenter to higher life forms. *Whatever feat higher life forms have made to transcend their animal counterparts is the manner in which higher life forms can understand the true epicenter with respect to itself.* By watching the chain of nature which leads to the epicenter, one will be able to understand the manner of differentiation between a higher life form and the epicenter. For instance, if a mammalian breed differentiates itself with a more distinct sexual role for its constituents, we would be safe to assume that the pathway from higher life forms towards the epicenter is a more distinct and elaborate sexual formation. The dynamic intimacy of the two counterparts is a distinct development of the mammal to the higher life form, and this would continue to be the case from the higher life form to the epicenter.

The Theos of Monotheism and the Theos of Religion

Monotheism is the notion of universality with the name Theos, yet the true epicenter is also being attributed as a Theos by religious identities. This is not a paradox within the notion of Theos but rather a lack of comprehension of religious identity. The identity is only in service to incorporate the more potent elements of nature, and even if we identify an epicenter, it will remain bound to the universal system. When the religious identity makes use of the word 'Theos' to describe this epicenter, it can lead to the assumption that the epicenter is removed from the universal system. This is not the case, for we are only concerned with the epicenter in consideration of the universal system which would need to recognize its potent parts.

When the religious identity makes use of Theos in this manner, we can justify their actions by recognizing this aspect. We have mentioned that universality must be distributed, which would have many quasi-universal systems under the umbrella of true universality. The epicenter is the most elevated quasi-universality under the rubric of true universality, although it will always remain a disturbed element from universality. The epicenter may interact to a very effective degree for which even higher life forms cannot fathom, yet it does not incorporate all the elements of nature which universality accomplishes. In religious doctrines, when Theos communicates, it is this quasi-universal epicenter from which it platforms. Even as it communicates with an intuition that transcends higher life forms, it is still under the rubric of the theory of monotheism.

Accordingly, from a monotheistic perspective, Theos does not speak from the universal platform as it would be a limitation of the true universality which transcends particular speech or individuation. Universality is in terms of all the elements that are known, as well as unknown, and cannot be defined on its own accord. The epicenter may communicate like a Theos to postulate designs that assist in asserting the universal system and the theory of monotheism. This Theos is an interactive center that transcends higher life form but falls short of complete universality. Therefore, whenever a doctrine refers to Theos in intention, action, or speech, they are referring to a potent interactive force that illuminates a strong degree of reality.

For instance, in the Abrahamic religions, Theos appeals to love thy neighbor, which understandably is a highly interactive statement. However, this is not a universal Theos to be attributed to monotheism, as this Theos is an example of ultimate universality, which comes to fruition when we attend to isolated elements of the universal picture. Therein, loving thy neighbor is not a universal dictum, since 'love', 'neighbor', and 'self' are secluded elements in the universal array of existence. Monotheism would only concern itself with having the universal reality being expressed within the universe.

We could essentially remove the traditional notion of Theos from the picture and work with the proposition since there is nothing beyond the scientific notion of monotheism. Therefore, the word monotheism as a proposition does more justice to the reality of it, than the term Theos does. The religious notion of Theos is analogous to the heart and brain, which are epicenters of the organism but will never gain the position of being the comprehensive structure. The higher life form is more than its most relevant parts and cannot be reduced to it. The epicenter can be viewed as a Theos, as we would view the psyche in regard to higher life forms, although when all things are considered; the epicenter and the psyche are components of a bigger system.

The fact is that the higher life form became a more interactive potency due to the endeavor of asserting the monotheistic theory. Having universality as an ideal would allow one to account for all the elements, especially those more interactive by innate nature. Monotheism is the cause which has people interact with the most potent interactive elements of nature. Taking an interest in the most interactive elements is allocated by pursuing universality in life, even though true universality would be something that would cause an individual to navigate away from any specific interactive element.

It is also the case that it is the cause for an individual to proximate nearer to the interactive elements, since within its fabric it contains a higher degree of universality than other elements of nature. This compels us to acknowledge that it causes one to neglect and subsequently overindulge from the most interactive elements, such as the religious identity's notion of Theos. As well, monotheism causes one to engage with the most interactive elements of nature, having encompassed within them a higher degree of universality than other elements of nature. Another way to understand this is that Theos of religious identity is a manifestation of perception. One would surely concede to the vulnerability of perception, being based on environmental and social constructs. Therefore, we would understand that any notion of Theos as an 'entity' has the capability of becoming an arena of fixating focus and indulgence.

Monotheism and Romantics

Romantics are engaging in a monotheistic notion by taking account of the most interactive elements of nature. When they become fixated or indulgent on those elements, they remove themselves from universality; an originating position which had caused them to begin their engagement. Thus, they can become transfixed in place, by not having a method that will alleviate their fixation with those interactive elements. This occurs due to a deficient recognition, that for whatever the elements of nature are offering, they are quasi-universal systems under a larger universality of existence.

Romantics may be removed from universality by other means, which is in the deliberate disregard for interactive elements that are beyond the higher life form mainframe. They may persistently ignore any romantic notion which is not grounded in clear individual and subjective experience. They are postulating that the higher life form is the absolute epicenter of all interactive elements, to eventually over-interact with certain elements; being that they continuously seek out inward experiences. This is coupled with the principle that the higher life form structure is inexhaustible, while even if we were to consider the absolute epicenter, it would have an exhaustible limit; being a part of a more complex universality.

Equality and Monotheism

The equality doctrine is a universal notion of existence, in which everything is interconnected and therefore equal in its connection to universality. Equality is disjointed from the monotheistic notion when equality is pursued without taking account of the more interactive elements of nature. What is occurring is that universality is becoming absolutely universal, being removed from nature and placed into a secluded unknown arena. Universality is becoming bigger than individuality and therefore does not have to integrate with social connections. Universality is being used as an element of a truly universal system with a facade that is universal. Higher life forms would be postulating the transcended nature of universality and using it for a doctrine of a particular nature. By making use of an inflexible system, one would use universality to alleviate the elements of contention within nature. This form of universality is a concealment for an idea which contains elements of quasi-universal understandings, while getting the prerogative of universal protection. *While true universality incorporates everything and excludes nothing, this merely includes the subtle differences between interactive elements.*

Pathological Thinking

The Terminology of Pathology

Freud (1923) defined pathological thinking as 'neurosis' and described it as
— "The symptom develops as a substitution for something else that has remained suppressed. Certain psychological experiences should normally have become so far elaborated that consciousness would have attained knowledge of them. This did not take place, however, but out of these interrupted and disturbed processes, imprisoned in the unconscious, the symptom arose."[2]

In principle, he states that a thought which did not obtain adequate attention will require a substitution for its place, these to become the uncomfortable symptoms of various psychological conditions. Those unattended thoughts are the prism for our discussion, as to what conditions must be met, all to not attend to a thought with adequate attention. Since thoughts cannot disappear into the abyss, to avoid them, they must be hidden from plain sight while remaining animated. We now requisite other thoughts that can conceal the unwanted substance. These unwanted thoughts preserve the animation by means of a bookmark which employs a dual position, on one side, to correlate conscious substance with its direct linkage to the dormant material, and the other, to avoid revealing the unwanted contents of the bookmarked information.

The internal dialogue is built in such a way that the conversation must flow in sequence despite the ensuing repression. To avoid certain thoughts, one must find auxiliary thoughts to carry on the internal conversation. We cannot simply prance over unwanted thoughts, having their part in the conversation albeit through differing thought material. For example, one who desires to avoid psyche material associated with death requires other thoughts to take its place, namely, thoughts of longevity, which correlate to the

---

[2] This quote is from *The Ego and the Id*, 1923.

animation of the dormant material, existing as its antonym and still transparent enough, for which death would not be inferred although gaining vitality from them. Any wise individual would understand that seeking longevity is vitalized by the looming demise; immortal beings would not divert the idea of longevity. With this example, we have also demonstrated how analysis can unearth pathological thinking. While the term 'neurosis' was adapted for psychological use by Freud, contemporary language has adopted other terms that are more descriptive of the experience of pathology.

As language is important for defining these concepts, let us find contemporary terminology. Some may call it a psyche *breakdown*, and quite understandably so, that through the personal experience of such symptoms, it would be sensed as such. This sense indicates the higher-life-form's optimal state, which is now at wit's end, with the ensuing structure to be breaking down; its entity becoming suboptimal. Another more clinical but descriptive form of pathology is *derangement*, where it is most noticed in the confines of formal sociality to be seeming to lack reason and coherence. Social forms of pathology are *insanity* and *madness*, both terms to describe how one would identify an individual in such a state. Social beings are *insane* or *mad,* amidst speaking to them we sense *derangement,* and when we subjectively experience it, we would ascribe it as a *breakdown*.

The Flow of Dialogue

While ignoring the pathways of thoughts to be considered pathological, so becomes the fixation with background thoughts. This fixation will surely reduce the natural flow of other thoughts, by demanding attention solely to these thoughts. We can define pathology as the diminishment of the fluid sequence of inner dialogue, either by neglect or fixation. Within pathological thinking, the mental landscape seeks to promote certain thoughts while dismissing or repressing others. The negative effect of pathology is noticed when thinking evolves into an internal struggle, in which each thought gains independent status.

When we consider the psyche to be a single unit then it must contain an unremitting dialogue. We can identify a wearisome dialogue to differ from one that is flowing and coherent. There is a conceptual requisite to maintain a functional inner dialogue, for when it becomes perturbed during dysfunctional dialogue, a component is interjected without acknowledging the wholesome completion of a coherent scheme.

However, it is also worth noting that some disruption within the inner dialogue can be normal and even beneficial, such when we intentionally interrupt our innate thoughts to re-evaluate, or problem solve. We could distinguish between functional and dysfunctional disruptions by the good faith in the interruption. Comparable to a courtroom, objections from counsel can be perceived as an interruption, while in such a context, interruptions are generally received as acceptable and even necessary to ensure that proceedings are fair and follow legal procedures. These are interruptions that are intended with the wholesome dialogue in mind, in which the body of the court is in agreement. This understanding of intentionality in accordance with interruptions can be applied to all pathological behavior.

Intentionality of Dialogue Disruption

Here are four examples to illustrate the theme. Pathological thinking can consist of imagining the worst-case scenario for believing it is likely to occur. This type of thinking can be intentionally wholesome when certain situations petition this way of thinking, such when handling dangerous equipment arranged on a regular basis. A second proposition for wholesome intentionality may involve limiting a perspective to only two extremes, with no opportunity for nuance or complexity. The circumstance is a period of action in which we cannot become distracted by the complexity of the situation. A third scenario would be to induce broad conclusions based on limited evidence or experience. In certain situations, it necessitates a hurried judgment for assuming others to be credulous. A fourth circumstance is when an individual assumes that everything which materializes is a reflection of themselves. When one wishes to self-reflect and perform dramatic changes to their character, a dramatized type of self-aggrandization is beneficial.

An instance of dysfunctional dialogue without the intentionality of wholesome dialogue is the case when a speaker possesses a patronizing tone. A hostile tone arises when one fixates upon a singular idea, discounting perspectives and considerations. Beneath the harshness lurks thoughts that are being overshadowed; thoughts that should participate in the conversation, secreted in the present statements. Refusing to consider alternative viewpoints or perspectives is pathological in that the natural considerations of the psyche are being suppressed to maintain the current viewpoints. This newfound independence of a thought pattern would confidently not wish to lose its independence, to be dissolved into the background. In effect, thoughts become entitled to the care that a wholesome higher life form enjoys. This contention of entitled thoughts results in significant dysfunction to the subjective experience.

Pathological Action

The inevitable result of pathology is that it leads to pathological action. This can be seen with either the compulsion to complete the task or the aversion to normalcy. We can take note of the psychotic state, which has lost touch with coherence in their patterns of thought, all preceding final activity of pathological nature. Pathological actions will be devoid of the prerequisites of sociality as even the psyche has lost influence of the ruminating pathological components. Psychotic actions may appear robotic and divorced from the higher life form aspect of personhood.

Social etiquette and standards will not be enough to prevent pathological actions from finding its course. Those social tools are a protection for individual temporality and are inadequate for the fixating focus that is characteristic of one who maintains certain thoughts to be independent in the spectrum of higher life form thinking. A less civilized society would rapidly rid such activity from the social arena, its initial pathological offense would be met with a severe response. Because we have civilized contemporary society, we defer our response to that of the civil authority, had that not been in place, we would quickly dispel pathological activity from our midst. This is theoretical, for in realistic terms, societies who are not civilized tend to allow pathological actions to be free; being in a degraded state in which each member seeks to possess the other for which even delinquency goes unnoticed. However, the potential of an uncivilized society to be pathologically free is greater than a civilized one.

We may like to perceive the subjective experience as wholly subjective while the objective realm to be exclusively objective. What occurs, rather, is a fusion of both experiences with an unclear distinction between the two. There is only so much chaotic subjective experience one can endure until it fuses with the objective world. Do not blame the actions that were enacted upon the society, rather blame an unattended subjective experience, which inevitably discharges to the objective world. We have come to notice actions of internal pathological activity, being thwarted in society, where its explanation can only be a manifest of some chaotic pathology. This might be our wonderment of these episodes, being unfamiliar to the other forms of delinquency. An arena of thought that can only gain insight once we have recognized a chaotic subjective experience, one in which the harmony of thoughts is not optimal.

Pathology and the Emotional Association with Thoughts

When the psyche is mentally functional, the notion of steady opposition might be comparable to having a single limb at odds with another. The psyche does not consider the possibility for thoughts to contend with each other, for they take great care for the expression of thought contained by their mental apparatus. However, there may be an emotional attachment or negative association with a particular thought pattern which has pathology become a natural occurrence. We may venture to say that pathology is the natural mode of being, in which avoiding such is against the currents of life.

We would naturally approach certain thoughts to be independent and sensible for extra devotion. Higher-life-forms fundamentally seek attachment so when a *good* thought arrives to the psyche, we would want to foster its attachment, while a *bad* thought would have us detach. This should not discourage the process; in a similar vein, we can state that animalistic behavior might be a natural deviation for higher life forms. The emotional burden attached to thoughts may be the central motivation for pathological thinking, with its promise of avoiding or overstimulating what is perceived as harmful or overly pleasurable.

Such is noticed in the notion of death, even as stimulating fixed thoughts alike the others, the emotional association is resilient. Thoughts in that department would be accredited as circumvention material, even as this would manifest to be pathological. Contrary to that, thoughts that ascertain towards longevity and immortality will be something that most would want to pamper.

The one who commits to circumventing the detrimental aspect of pathology will allow thoughts concerning death to be heard as they are. Such thinking will bring depressive states with existential dread, still, the functional psyche will not overlook these thoughts and their experiences. We may observe that most people will be tasking themselves with activity so as to avoid an existential crisis. However, the burden of the emotional bundle should not influence the delegation of those thoughts. No thoughts should be deemed inappropriate by their fundamental nature, nor should other thoughts be overly fixated upon for their provisions.

This perspective of thought observes all psyche activity as significant and would not allow the neglect of a partiality of its components. They find thoughts to be further consecrated than the associated emotional experiences; being that emotion is the heir of thoughts and not independent of itself. We could stipulate arguments to defend emotions as independent, worthy of their distinctive regard. Thus, a new term for pathology may be obligatory, contained by the domain of emotion, where the neglect or omission of certain emotions doesn't allow a natural sequence of feeling to take place. For the sake of deviation from this discussion, let us adhere to the idea that emotions are the heir of thoughts and therefore should be secondary for a pathological discussion. If we can find forms of thinking within every emotion, whereas we cannot find emotion in every pattern of thought, we can deduce that emotion is a derivative of thought.

Identity of Thoughts

The process of separable thinking and its particular patterns of thought can be identified as either independent or dependent on its biological structure. How we view strains of thought surrounded by a higher-life-form framework would dictate how we utilize the psyche and its contents. Identification is essentially the process of how we use and experience thoughts. As per the identity of a professional will determine much of their persona when dealing with sociality, so does the identification of thoughts that are differentiated from the body to affect thinking itself.

As thoughts are contained within an organic structure, we must identify thoughts in reference to personhood as a whole. Just as we identify the arm to be a part of the body, we must find the identity of the thought process within the sociality of the organic structure. The limb is outwardly a part of the body, and we relatively do not strain with another possible identity. We can identify a limb to be independent of biological material although such discerning would be difficult to satisfy the psyche; evidently seeing its dependence on the body. A doctor might identify their arm to be an instrument of healing, while a tailor, an instrument of weaving, still one must acquiesce its bond to the body and the corresponding psyche. The doctor does not think the arm brings healing, but rather the body serves its physical abilities while the psyche dictates its direction towards healing. The doctor can enjoy a sub-identity of the arm, being an instrument of healing, and may experience the arm in that vein, yet it is understood to be under the rubric of a meta-identity — dependent on the body and psyche. There would be a trend of conceit if the doctor was adamant that the arm is an instrument of healing without accounting for its encompassing identity. Ultimately, the meta-identity should dominate the overall experience of the arm, being that it is fundamentally truer than 'instrument of healing'.

When identifying thoughts as independent of the biological higher-life-form, it paves the way toward contention between thoughts. The contention contracts certain thoughts while over-attending to other thoughts, which is how contending thoughts evolve to be pathological. On one hand, thoughts are so influential of an experience that we can assume them to have "a psyche of their own." Biologically, it is clear that thoughts do not become independent from their higher-life-form mainframe. Moreover, it is assumed that the psyche is somehow transcendent to the body and its limitations. Therefore, we must be austere on such assumptions and recognize thoughts to be intermingled in the mesh of biology and not beyond its biological limits. For the other extreme, thoughts are physically invisible and can be assumed to be so insignificant which may lose their recognition as an entity within the biological structure, e.g., soul. So that we contain both the inspiration to deem psyche contents as a prevailing entity of its own, and accompanying contents which we are not fond of, to be presumed insignificant; we sort out the evidence for either position according to the will of that contention.

Entity versus Dependents

When one identifies thoughts as independent from the body, being external, they can now employ contentious sentiment with each other. The fabric elements of our biological structure that identify as united with the organic system do not contend with each other. This is because they are inherently identified within the structure and would not be presumed as an external entity. There is a unifying force within the organization which does not allow such variance to arise. The ostensible perspective of our organic system is that the limbs are distinct parts of a unifying structure. Even if we can formulate a conceptual argument contrary to this premise, physical action that performs its task in unison denotes a unified character.

This understanding becomes more complicated when we approach the organic structure and the concealed phenomena within the psyche. Since the psyche is obscured, we can formulate argumentation which may assert thought to be independent of the organic organization. With abstract logic, we can disengage from this unification so that we can isolate one of its parts, specifically the psyche and its contents. Thus, the one who abstracts may postulate that each part of the body is in service to itself and does not engage in that unity. This claim would be supported by the fact that all organisms are a unified entity of their own; each having their unique organized structure. The problem with this conceptualization is that our reality is embedded within a larger entity, that of nature. Nature would be the overall body, and individual would only constitute a limb upon that structure. As all phenomena is both an organization of its own and a part of a larger organization, this necessitates a distinction. For what shall be categorized as an entity and what shall be considered as a dependent on another entity?

Our Approach of what Constitutes an Entity

Even as the body is dependent on nature akin to the limb being dependent on the body, we should consider individual existence to be an entity. For this discussion about the psyche and its performance, we are in search of the study for higher life forms, so that we will name the individual as the entity while the subcomponents as dependents. When one considers dissecting anything, one must place emphasis on that as the entity, while considering its components as dependents. To adequately understand a structure, allowing too much information into purview we will get distracted. We do wish to explore cosmic reality or delve into the molecular level, just as sociality and its studies we do not deal with the vastness of space or the microscopic particles, so we will not engage in those arenas.

We will take the middle ground, placing higher life forms at its epicenter. We will not perceive our existence as a mere dependent of nature, a sentiment that corresponds to the perspective of our limbs in reference to our bodies. Moreover, we will not perceive the various organisms presiding in our corporeal structure to be independent entities deserving of personal attention. This discussion can be expanded with philosophical inquiry but deviates from our study of pathological thinking. Despite all the argumentation, we would never disengage from identifying ourselves as a certain unified entity. Even if we attempt such an assignment, the results will lead to discord between our limbs. Suffice it to say, there is an intuitive agreement that everything must be considered unified and singular without the possibility of logical contradiction.

It remains to be seen if an individual can rationally create discord between body parts. At least from a physical vantage point it has been proven, as we see from research which has been emphasized by McGilchrist (2010), when the "right hemisphere is not functioning properly, the left hemisphere may actually deny having anything to do with a body part which does not seem to be working according to the left hemisphere's instructions."[3] Although McGilchrist's objective of asserting a major demarcation at play between the two hemispheres, for our discussion, it appears that the contents of the psyche should be considered alike their corresponding limbs. They too are biological components of the higher life form, and they too carry their physical characteristics.

Preliminary Thought Patterns

To assume that every piece of knowledge in regard to our psyche can be measured numerically is incomplete. Some pieces of knowledge are

---

[3] "Patients will report that the hand 'doesn't belong to me' or even that it belongs to the person in the next bed, or speak of it as if made of plastic. One patient complained that there was a dead hand in his bed. A male patient thought the arm must belong to a woman in bed with him; another complained that there was a child in the bed, on his left. Yet another was convinced that the nurses had bundled up his arm with the dirty laundry and sent it away to be washed.

One patient believed quite firmly that the paralyzed arm belonged to her mother, though in all other respects her conversation was quite normal. A patient described by Lhermitte showed no concern and was positively euphoric, despite being paralyzed down his left side: 'it seemed as if the entire left-hand side of his body had disappeared from his consciousness and from his psychic life'. Three days later, however, this patient reports that from time to time an alien hand, which disturbs and annoys him, comes and places itself on his chest: he says 'this hand presses on my tummy and chokes me'. 'This hand bothers me', he says again, 'it doesn't belong to me, and 'I'm afraid it might thump me.'"

McGilchrist, Iain, *The Master and His Emissary*, Ch. 2, 2010.

fundamental concepts. These concepts can influence the majority of the psyche and deserve serious attention. The psyche should be viewed as layers so that its elementary layers influence its outer layers. A child might see a bus and see a moving object while a mature person would perceive it as a riding object. Finally, a development in the mature stage will perceive the bus as a way to get places. The earlier frame: the bus being a moving object, will always influence the advanced layers of comprehension so that a bus mechanic will still rely on that earlier frame in the advanced conception of a bus.

When we decide to entertain a discussion about moving objects, this childhood concept will take precedence. The conception of the bus began from this, and so we cannot remove that preconception from the present moment. The intellectually stimulating conversation about moving objects would be influenced by the conception of the bus as a 'riding object' and its later forms of 'a way to get places'. For instance, we may understand movement in concert with our internal development in its ability to transcend. This conception is associated with our childlike perception of moving objects and will also connect to the conception of riding objects. Thus, the conception of a 'way to get places' will be furthered with an internal objective that brings about such movement; that a clear vision and objective are the catalysts for such movement. Alternatively, the conception of 'a way to get places' will be a component of the much later intellectual discussion. With deliberate analysis, we can find the strings that mend the immature conception to this mature one.

The former layers of perception will dominate the landscape of the psyche for all of life. The rudimentary components of our makeup will also dominate the landscape as they are interconnected with our perception, thus, the concept of sexuality will always play a significant role in all knowledge that can be assessed. Another example would be self-preservation, which will demonstrate its fundamental nature in all of psychology. In how we perceive our thoughts will be one such fundamental layer and pathology will offer insight into all these later conceptions.

An Etymological Explanation for Pathology

Let us elaborate on the basis of pathological thinking. When details matter, it is surely in the realm of complex conditions that the details become the core of a clear and coherent exposition. Observe the word itself, although etymologically incorrect, pathology contains the word 'path', describing the compulsion of a directed approach to thinking—disallowing external deterrents to diminish its strength. The word path can be understood in pathways, in which groupings of thought patterns travel in the direction of a spotlight; the attentive conscious psyche. These groupings are formed by reduced or incoherent thoughts that ascend to the conscious compartment by its driving forces and objective. Pathology would be an adherence to certain pathways either in a fixation or repressive manner. Thoughts can be regarded as pathways since there is an infinite number of thoughts that could be approached, the choice of this particular one is always against the competing background of the others. The misfortune comes when a single pattern of thought takes charge into the conscious. In neuroscience, the perspective of thought is observed as neural pathways which only lends itself to this definition.

Alternatively, if the spotlight of attention is expended to diminish patterns of thought which would naturally enter the spotlight, we must use methods of coercion and fear to banish that pathway from lingering in the attention-sphere. This is where symptoms usually arise, as those methods can comprise unwanted results for the overall experience. The same applies to the compulsion toward specific thoughts, of using both methods of coercion and deception. Coercion: to keep other thoughts at bay while these thoughts remain in attention. Deception: to intellectually contend the need of these thoughts to be attended to. The one who wants to experience longevity will deceive the psyche of their aging process to keep the thoughts of longevity in place. They will also require a method to diminish natural thoughts of death through coercion of sorts.

Thoughts as being Interconnected

Another benefit for cogitating thoughts as pathways is signifying the constitution to be based on antecedent patterns of thoughts but also must continue to complementary paths. *All roads must lead to all roads.* It becomes imperative to not disengage specific thoughts from their internal dialogical bearing. In obtaining an adequate definition of pathology, we must perceive thoughts as part of an internal dialogue. Thoughts are never impartial, being in a continuous motion. Even when we segregate thoughts, we are only extrapolating pieces of a sequence and must remember the substructure is that all sequential thought patterns are related. Shouldn't symptoms in unwholesome thinking be the evidence, which in the attempts to halt a harmonious succession of thinking, we must use grave emotional methods to obtain that objective?

We cannot disband thoughts without a painstaking process which includes many unwanted symptoms to achieve its objective. If we could trim pieces of thought, we would not be experiencing disruption in the process. Only in recognizing that internal dialogue is layered upon a sequence of a single conversation can we make sense of pathology. The name pathology bears that mark of disturbing the conversation with a definite topic, becoming 'path'oligized. We cannot contemplate a set of thoughts as being exclusive, all without a previous set of thoughts that allows their arrival.

This may seem questionable since we think of ourselves as autonomous in our thought patterns with the ability to rush in whatever we desire to think. Take whatever thought you may be thinking and analyze its contextual arrival. Even if you compulsorily decide on a particular thought, with some analysis you will find the pathways which lead you there. With this realization, one may think internal conversation is not available for one's influence or control. For even if this book arose in your reading opportunity through contextual thoughts for which you cannot control, you could attentively absorb the contents and indeed will influence the direction of subsequent mental events. The attention of experience is in the realm of genuine influence, for the quality does not have specific pathways, as there is some legroom between the neural paths and the adherence of them. One couldn't merely seek a certain education, rooted in subjective pathways of thought and environmental dependencies, rather the adherence to the quality of that education is in the realm of unpredictable personhood.

Pathology and Coherence

Having a thought arise without a rational path from its predecessor can also be considered pathological. Every thought retains a cohort of predecessors, granting that on the occasion for which it doesn't maintain coherence it would be considered pathological. We are beginning to understand that pathology is closely related to coherence. To print out a transcript of the internal dialogue of one engaging in pathological thinking, we would find incoherent trends. It may be unlikely to obtain a transcript of pathology without being bothered by its incoherence, the question of only the method of emphasis on subconscious patterns to be included in this transcript, for which it would soften the incoherence accordingly.

The core disruption that produces pathology is the disparity of perspective that renders the process of thought to be in line with a real conversation. We may perhaps forget this analysis and proceed to the practice of attending to the subconscious thought patterns, skipping the crucial steps of a comprehensive study of pathology. We want to dissociate from the intention of the clinicians and patients, for only dispelling unwanted symptoms of pathology. We genuinely want to understand psyche parameters, deserving attention beyond symptom diminishment.

All the same, when an individual chooses to think about the weather affecting another continent, all with no coherent correlation, would be considered engaging in pathological activity. Surely there is a path to uncover which led them to that thought; and with enough analysis we may find that they saw the color *red*, an association to that continent, making sensible that correlation. The fissure from the associative connection to an intimate thought pertaining to the weather begs the question of its origin. Especially considering the value asset of a thought entering the spotlight of consciousness, with an infinite number of thoughts contesting its temporal space. If we had converted this internal thought process into a conversation, the other party would appear perplexed by the question of weather, having only mentioned the continent in association with the color red. The transcript of that fissure would dictate where the pathology is to be found, which may be a fixation with the color *red* which has the weather closely related. For if *red* was veritably a family member, then inquiring about the weather becomes coherent. Why does color take the position as intimate as family members, considering that indeed family members are contesting that space of attention? Consequently, it may be a primary sexual memory in which the color *red* was its theme. Being a wearisome event, the psyche did not allow the contents to become a part of the expected internal conversation. The factors that contribute to repression are numerous and can range from societal pressure to familial guilt.

Red is taking the place of the sexual memory, and sexuality is surely an intimate part of a higher life form. The fixation for dispelling the sexual experience from its natural flow is the juncture of pathology. Further discussion will unearth the deep reasons for this. Still, we can identify the trend of pathology in a thought process, which creates an internal dialogue that would be incoherent if expressed. Surely, with this supplementary information, it becomes coherent, but then again it was not included in the conscious conversation. So, we can say that subconsciously there is no pathology, as the ground level can never become incoherent because the conversation is fundamentally singular. *Consciousness is the realm of pathology, just as coherence is in the realm of spoken words.*

Pathology by way of Analogy – Parts of a Whole

Allow me to frame the individualistic condition through this particular framework — parts of a whole, in which each component seeks to be incorporated into the whole. Moreover, the whole seeks unity without overemphasizing any single component. The reason for the aversion of a particular component is that it would threaten the harmony of the whole. Although this is a reductionist view, its simplicity can offer us insight into the mental experience, in addition, we must remember that obtaining the key conditions of our psyche is quite challenging. To engage in any productive dialogue of such complex systems, we will benefit by generalizing to approximating aspects that are simple and digestible, even as it doesn't align with objective reality.

Therefore, we can define pathology in this framework — the components *desiring* to be considered the whole itself. In a similar vein, one who is congratulatory will instinctively desire to maintain certain characteristics as a part of their whole identity. They will not consider the partiality of the characteristics they are congratulatory about, expanding the specifics to become the entirety of personhood through the process of identification.

The pathway towards overemphasizing a single component can occur for a variety of reasons, one being the overconfidence of the component. For example, one believes their attribute to be factual to the extent that it becomes a perceived version of selfhood. They are approaching the attribute without recognizing the conditions for which it is encompassed by. Surely, a particular component is a moderate part of personhood, but we are always unaware to what degree, although we can be cognizant that no component can be attributed to the entire entity. Another theme derived from this analogy is that a component is a sort of entity and cannot be unheeded as irrelevant information. The entity cannot function without its components, so that each component is relevant to the expression of the entire entity.

Another factor that can be attributed to overemphasizing a component is philosophical resistance. Since each component contains the attributes of the whole entity for which the entity is dependent, the component can be branded as the whole. Furthermore, at each moment, only a single thought can be showcased in the spotlight of consciousness, maintaining that components are at least momentarily considered the whole. To answer the latter, we may say that personhood or all entities are phenomena that run through time, and we must take that into account. As thoughts move in and out of the spotlight, we cannot halt the clock to use that moment as the overarching narrative of personhood. We must take into account all the moments at our disposal if we are to label an entity in accurate proportions. Secondly, a component contains attributes of the entire entity but still cannot take the place of the entire entity from which it stems. We can only entertain the component because of the entity which it is embedded so that the component is severely dependent on the entity for its expression. There is an inter-reliant relationship which prevents either the whole entity from oppressing the component or from the component overhauling the whole enterprise.

Another derivative we can gain from this analogy is the acknowledgment that there must be a flow from one component to another. By definition of an 'entity and its components' there must be more than a single component. Transpiring that components are numerous, continuous connections must be made which are fluid between its successions from one component to another.

Even as we can't always define components in realistic terms, whatever that characteristic may be, we could still surmise its parameters.

Firstly, it can never be the whole entity, secondly, it can never be irrelevant material, and thirdly, it must naturally flow in and out of the spotlight of consciousness. In other terms, the whole cannot tyrannize, the parts cannot overthrow the establishment, and there must be communication of all its parts. Therefore, a component that becomes pathological would not allow for other components to be expressed as a part of the whole. This is "a replacement of the father and the ousting of the brothers' scenario." Pathological behavior requires that the father be replaced and to repress the voice of the brothers, essentially to take the role of domineering figure. Freud analogizes this phenomenon as a "state within a state," where the component becomes pathological when existing as an autonomous entity within the larger whole.

Pathology by way of Analogy – Organization Analogy

Consider a commercial enterprise, one with a substantial amount of employee activity and a hierarchical structure for which it depends upon. The highest executive of the enterprise must offer their instructions so that they will filter upon each level without having the instruction diluted or left unfulfilled. Such is not an easy task as one must recognize the nature of transmission from the first level to the subordinate. While the first level only needs to relay the information to the next, the realistic implementation at the lower levels of the organization would be difficult for an executive to anticipate. Though the first juncture of transmission is via speech, the last point of this transmission is via implementation. A worded idea and its practical realization are fundamentally different, just as this text is a collection of worded ideas for which the implementation will be altered and modified.

By understanding the detriment of pathological thinking to then finding such a pattern is vastly different than correcting its course. The clinical fields that aim to correct the results of pathology may take different approaches. We can notice a trend of pathology between ideas and their implementation due to their programmed difference, and we can easily construe an idea to be the same as its stage of implementation. The idea of liberty can be grouped together with its stage of implementation becoming the pathological foreground; being compelled together even as they are apart.

Another reason for the difficulty of transmission is that each component of the organization must act in accordance with its role as a component. We have established that a component is required to be a definite part of the whole; with autonomy and influence over the whole. This control of the whole cannot go so far since the component assumes the role of the whole, or that the component neglects their status as a participating member of the whole. Finally, this component must facilitate a smooth transition from themselves to others and from others to them. This places the executive in a precarious position, where the instruction should not fail in the transition from one member to another. Moreover, it doesn't offer too much power to the component or belittle the component's participation in the objective. Pathology appears when through the transmission of the instruction, instead of each participant engaging in their internal critical thinking to incorporate the basis of the instruction, it is received only for the purpose of being implemented, with the simple basis of completing the objective. So that the components of the whole entity are not being experienced as a component of the entity's body, in which the component becomes "a state within a state." At the level of the organization, we can see pathology appear, where the active voice of the members is either stifled or overreaching, resulting in a production that does not flow seamlessly from the executive to the end product. Instead, gaps in the transmission can be realized at the production level. These gaps are members who are not producing from the perspective of the company, instead are deriving results from thinking that do not match the general conversation of the organization.

Pathology by way of Analogy – Biological Analogy

If a social organization is too abstract to parallel intricacies within the psyche, we can use our inborn organism as a more subtle example. Within biology, we can illustrate this point, for body parts unify to become a unified entity, so that each particular segment seeks to belong to the unified entity. Subsequently, the unified entity seeks to be unified as a whole without neglecting or incorporating parts to be beyond its branding. The arm is an entity in its peculiar right, yet it is subservient to the body. Still, the unified body seeks to be unified under a single authority. Pathology would arise when one particular body part dominates the others, dispelling the adequate expressions of the other parts. This would manifest as the arm pursuing all the attention without allowing the legs, for instance, to take a role in its service to the unified entity.

Pathology, in this context can be defined as overestimating or underestimating a component from its encompassing whole. The estimation of a particular part is only in its value accorded to its role in the setting of a systemic structure. We do not evaluate an arm in isolation, without the consideration of its place in the categorization of the body. If we do choose to make an objective estimation of the arm, without taking note of the system it is dependent on, we enter the realm of abstract reasoning. Abstract inquiry always begs the enquiry to what relevance for the analysis of a component, one embellished in its characteristic solitude, to help in the progress of a system or structure.

For in practical terms, whatever knowledge is uncovered, say the study of fingerprinting, would always result in a settled impact in the entirety of the system. We don't identify the hands of delinquents; we identify their wholesome stature derived from a component of them. This claim could be challenged by pointing out that disciplined research on specialized regions of an organism has subsequently led to significant medical breakthroughs. However, the benefit would only be useful for the totality of the organism. For prosthetics that don't adequately contribute to the whole entity of the body, and might we say of personhood, would be unserviceable. We would not treat a region of the body when the circumstance would fail for the entirety of personhood or organism.

It may appear that the act of underestimating a component would release its confinement from participating in the whole entity but would not go so far as to be a contestant to pathology. On closer examination, with both the example of the body and of the organization, for when either a body part or an employee is underestimated, all the while, at the present moment still tasked with participating, whatever input they do engage will be pathological; for the reason that they are disengaged from the entity yet still participating in the enterprise.

Let us apply this comprehension to the process of thought, considering each particular thought to be a component of a unified entity. Each thought, its pathways, its memories, and associations are to be labeled as a component of that whole. We are not accustomed to labeling such minuscule creatures as components, nevertheless, we are tasked to consider a thought to be an entity no less than a limb. Imagining that every coherent thought is a sole entity within a broader entity, that these thoughts are not limited conscious substance which has the attribute of being dated into forgotten memory or repressed into the subconscious. They are considered a component because at one point in the progression of growth, these thoughts were relevant as conscious and animated thoughts. They remain such and cannot be removed as a component in the overall entity of the psyche. The entire body of thought is formed to include all sentient thoughts that have ruminated from infancy till present-day. Whereas within an organization, members could always be removed, thoughts are more analogous to the organism, in which they remain part of the inherent nature of the entity. To remove a thought from the organization can only be accomplished by discourse; to weaken its relevance or to substitute it.

Moreover, there can be an array of thoughts that wish to be voiced within the psyche, while the organism commands to be unified as a singular entity. Instead of perceiving thoughts as a competition of conscious relevance, understand them as we would a functional organization where the competition is mutual and co-engineered. Each member of the establishment is relevant to the whole body, negating another member would coincidentally negate the entity; a whole-body dependent on both competitors. Thus, competition can be rendered as neglecting oneself; competition of thoughts can be deciphered as neglecting oneself.

Monotheism

Monotheism, or the principle of a categorical Theos, asserts that all entities, including the associations between thoughts, are part of a primary collective. This is the manner in which it opposes pathology, in that it does not allow seclusion to the structure of thinking, for it wholly unifies to a single point, especially foreign to the psyche domain. Monotheism perceives the external realm as universal and interdependent, for every conceivable conception develops to be interconnected or interdisciplinary.

To illustrate, the notion of *war* would consist of a dynamism and imitative experience which is composed of the same source, even with that of healing. Through the interaction of researching *war* one adjoins to another discipline, namely that of healing; ostensibly its opposite. All notions of *war* require healing measures, in the form of field hospitals and medical combatants, including the strategic assessments of combat, undeniably taking health risk into account. When approaching a locale, one may inquire about the availability of health measures or resources in those geographical settings. Furthermore, in the effort of *war*, one may need to decide if the strategic objective is to mend the wounds or continue the general combat. The resulting analysis is that the research of *war* warrants a coinciding study of medicine. This applies to every discipline, which upon a certain degree of depth can or will transition to any other discipline or conceptual framework of the psyche.

Alternatively, one who studies medicine may view the research to be secluded from the scholarship of *war*. That is, until one realizes that injury and the vast effects of violence directly result in the field of medicine. Neuroscience was cemented in the treatment and assessment of brain damage, a direct causality from the battlefield. A doctor must preserve certain knowledge concerning *war* to assess the situations, the subsequent aftermath of *war*, and discover the balance between safety and health. Should the doctor attend to these patients in moderate condition, while worse casualties ensue from another form of violence? What will the preparatory measures be for the resulting injuries?

A component of *war* and its violence continues to move forward into hospitals. The doctor will be called, second to the soldier on the battlefield, and thus will be interconnected to that field of study. What seems ironic is that medical personnel may carry weapons, being closely associated with that realm. Moreover, the clinician studies the anatomical structure in a microscopic manner, no different than the combatant for the adverse objective in inflicting a lethal wound.

One who engages in the various disciplines under the rubric of 'humanities' will naturally encroach on all parallel disciplines which is appropriate to the access of subtly and nuance that are interchangeable in those different domains. When one identifies beauty within the concept of healing, or as we have noted with many medieval paintings; the beauty of *war*, the subject material will necessitate a correlating study of those disciplines. How would a painter who did not study *war* depict the beauty of *war*? Without the knowledge of medicine, how would one find the designs of beauty around them?

Only with a deep analysis of the concepts will one be able to identify and depict the beauty of each. We can reverse the scenario, for the art of medicine, without taking into account the beauty that lies behind it, will find a less palatable approach to the patient. The contemporary era is quite remarkable in its fashion of sub-standards for beauty within the field of medicine. While one who is trained in warfare will find a certain advancement in their abilities when they envision the battlefield from the vantage of the artist. Instead of becoming engrossed in underdeveloped narratives which are the central cause for a loss of morale, they would maintain the sentiment expressed in the well-known paintings of *war*, 'a sense of glory'.

Monotheism and Disciplines

Each discipline, as long as it remains insulated from other disciplines, will dissipate according to its inborn disintegration. Ostensibly, it won't produce much harm when the geologist takes no notice of the text scholar. However, for a prolonged duration, one will find the discipline to be circumventing much material that would provide acumen, even when it is beyond its margins. Without accounting for the various disciplines that allow for a specific discipline, in due course it will lack adequate breadth or comprehensive scope.

The study of medicine, without accounting for the traditional or holistic measures, forms a quarantined island that deteriorates the overall study. The immense volume of knowledge of the traditional body is condensed to permit an emphasis on advanced remedies. These are strict parameters imposed on the study of medicine, which without venturing beyond, becomes a sterile system. In essence, knowledge which does not expand beyond disciplinary parameters, eventually withers away. On the contrary, knowledge which only seeks to be interdisciplinary becomes either a formation that is atypical of a cult or lost to coherence. To form an absolute interdisciplinary discipline will require the departure from normal social interactivity, as regular sociality cannot relate to the curated discipline; requiring a new language that is only articulated by those within that domain.

Even within each discipline, such as the study of medicine, one would require many other forms of knowledge to accurately produce healing. To identify a symptom, a doctor would be required to contrast the condition to a database of knowledge that correlates to the symptom. The contrast between the two, the symptom and its correlation in the database, would require a method that medical knowledge does not offer. The specialist would need to use a method of rationality and deduction to identify the pathway of healing. An exceptional clinician who lacks logic and rationality would be antithetical to proper healing. As a matter of fact, we may say, more important than the knowledge of medicine is rationality and comprehension. Immense knowledge of medicine may be harmful to the concluding results owed to the misuse of rationality on the subject of the knowledge. A physician must have the wisdom to know when to burden the patient or when to reserve treatment to allow the environmental course to coexist. We would never accept that a doctor ought to continuously identify problems, just as we wouldn't want any other discipline to do so. Astuteness would be the discipline that allows the doctor to make the correct choices for healing.

Within the knowledge of medicine itself, such as understanding that penicillin mold can heal bacterial infections, obliges the distinct discipline that accounts for penicillin mold. The knowledge of medicine itself requires that one understand the properties of mold owed to its effect on bacteria. The study of mold is not part of the study of medicine, yet to recognize its medicinal properties one must gain a distinctive knowledge of mold. Even as this can be outsourced to other professionals, a specialist who doesn't take pledge for the discipline of mycology will not be cognizant of the substance that is ultimately administered to the patient. Every quantity of medicinal knowledge will be associated with supplementary disciplines and their subsequent vehicles of knowledge.

That being the case, consider the ancient Egyptians, for they maintained a Theos for *mold* while also conserving a Theos for *healing*. It would be a nonstarter to entertain the scientific notion that mold, ingested, would induce healing, as each notion is derived from a contradictory foundation. Even if we were to communicate that mold can heal bacterial growth, they would not practice such medicine, as per the Theos of *mold* does not interact with the Theos of *healing*; Sekhmet. That is, unless they unite them through a sort of myth that would allow the two to synthesize, consenting the adjacent mortal creatures to connect these two metaphysical properties; not a common mythological occurrence until we encounter the Hellenistic age.

From these examples, we can deduce that no discipline resides in a particular niche, one which does not interact with coinciding disciplines. The notion of monotheism postures that the study of *war* and the study of *medicine* are derivatives of the equivalent energy and source. This allows for the integration between the two, which previously would not have been able to be entertained. The ancient Egyptians believed that Sekhmet, the Theos of *war* and *healing*, was of a particular source, while Hathor, the Theos of *love* and *beauty* was of another source. Indeed, this was the circumstance, and *war* was not a central theme of beauty for the society of ancient Egypt. Military depictions primarily highlighted Pharaoh's successful defense or victories rather than glorifying *war*. The familiarity of the element *beauty* and the element of *war* could not be diverted as a categorical source. Consequently, they would need to retreat away from integrating the somewhat natural experience of the manifestation of *beauty* within *war*. *War* is of a particular Theos and beauty, another; their interaction, whatever it may be in sentiment is not unified, so that there will be no distinct space that encompasses them.

Existential Connection to Aspects of Nature

This principle is the foundation for concepts like *nature* and *universe*. To group the entire apparatus of various phenomena which seem characteristically distinctive is something that can only be accomplished by a unifying measure. Especially considering how we are existentially invested in particular aspects of nature, further predisposing towards accrediting those elements to be secluded from the rest. Comparable to recognizing an intimate family member to be of the same dynamic source as an unfamiliar stranger. Even as we acknowledge the unified sociality of higher life forms, contained by the intimate setting, one would not consider a stranger to participate with corresponding esteem and intimacy. In a general sense, the most transparent change of a stranger may go unnoticed, whereas for an intimate member the impact could be profound, altering their respective self-perception.[4]

The natural inclination is censorship to the spanning of all possible aspects under the rubric of a universe, associating the divergent degrees of connection to the explicit sources that are idiosyncratically rooted to that degree of intimacy. To withdraw from the premise would require opposing the senses

---

[4] Steinhart, E., *On the number of gods*, International Journal for Philosophy of Religion — "Ordinal polytheism suggests a number of gods proportional to the ordinal, with each god actualizing the best universe(s) in the n-th level of an axiological hierarchy of possible universes."

and posture their ostensible complexity and diversity to be of the same element, or in the case of senses — to be the same rooted sense or emotional source. Our experience of nature is divisive and the inclination towards a single portion would be so unlike another, eliciting a certain indifference, to engender an existential leap for the ability to attribute them to a categorical foundation.

The Collective as a Prerequisite to Monotheism

Immediately, we are actuated into a unity by the subjective aim of our inborn individuality within all of this content. If nature is to be *nature*, then individuality can simply be a part of nature, deprived of any recognition of existence at the center of or for anything. To decentralize the individual comes at a loss of individuality and relation. Therefore, we are compelled to discuss monotheism from the vantage of the communal body, which allows one to put aside individuality to feasibly entertain the theory. Thus, the collective sanctions us to transcend individual centrality to participate in the complexity of the 'average higher-life-form' and integrate that information within the individual state. By presenting as a scientific theory, monotheism is liable to enter from a collective body of work and its traditional parameters, hereafter, which individuals can partake.

We would need a form of centrality for this decentralized theory. Consequently, one partakes in a compartmentalized version of monotheism. This would indicate that the demonstrative connection with the intimate social member will be, in the meantime, treated as secluded from affairs. The monotheistic version will stand adjacent to the unified experience of that specific connection, which reflects on many subsequent layers. Instead of grouping higher life forms into a cluster, the individual connection will be magnified and recognized for the monotheistic tendencies within it. That is in the interim, since it is only a compartmentalization of a stricter form of monotheism which will inevitably assert that there is such a thing as a wholesome 'higher-life-form'.

Individualism and Monotheism

By its definition, the individualistic emotional connection, when in purview, will be making use of monotheism in a sternly individualistic sense. That is, polytheism manifests when certain emotional connections are treated as separate from the rest. What comes to mind is vengeance, which receives a coupled sentiment only to disregard the rest from consideration. We may want to attribute a more compartmentalized version of monotheism for vengeance, which seeks the wholeness of a single emotion. However, the keen observer would notice the vengeful ones are adamant in their position.

The individual who mandates complete absorption of a singular connection will mull it over until it becomes exhausted, which at that point, will eventually relinquish the inquiry. They will not allow this natural juncture of exhaustion to take effect and will undertake polytheistic tendencies by supposing that it is the sole reality of existence.

We derive a fundamental difference between monotheism and polytheism, between the availability to exhaust a supposition or to be unavailable. For monotheism, even with the momentous appeals for compartmentalization, when overstimulated, one will entreat or retreat to a different perspective of the unified vastness. While for polytheism, no juncture can be designated as overstimulated or exhausted, being considered the only reality of existence. The justification for when an individual exhausts the relenting attention to a singular point is not because 'reality' contains more than its substance, instead, the premise of a higher-life-form has stretched its limits in partaking with that dosage of reality.

Vengeance and Polytheism

The vengeful one can justify the capability of sleep because they recognize the limits of their biological system rather than reality being questioned. What seems peculiar is that if there is an eventual waning of the vengeful state, one will conjure another justification which permits them to switch away from it. Otherwise, to suppose that reality became more wholesome than that vengeful state; differing from this premise to being rather unable for a variety of reasons to manage that full reality, having them settle for another perspective.

We would acknowledge this when the opportunity for vengeance ascends again and are drawn towards complete vigor as if they had not let go for a duration. This is *Hamlet's* fundamental problem, never letting go of the worldview which assumes that particular vengeance to be the only reality. He can manage in the meanwhile, only by the self-perception that he must relinquish this reality due to his innate inability to perform it.

When the situation arises to perform vengeance, he leaps from behind the "curtain" without any rationality. The reality which has been tucked away, one which he felt inferior towards, is again available to be interacted with. The faults made in the mistaken killings were directly due to the rashness of having been away from that reality while indeed only managing despite that simmering vengeful reality to at once to be fully confronted by it. The swift switch caused the psyche to be unable to digest the information, other than having the opportunity to partake in that failed reality once again; who wouldn't resist such an offer? This is why Hamlet is the one struggling to make sense of his existence, for he has reserved reality to be of a certain vengeful kind, and in the intermedium, he is inferior to that reality.

Negativism originates from a certain polytheism which brands the worldview to be only of a certain kind, overwhelming the individual into a sub-existent state. While for the monotheistic tendency, no experience can be considered a composite picture of reality; there is always the monotheistic backdrop behind whatever centrality is found in a particular moment. Within the entirety of the universe as demanded of monotheism, one would give way from this reality to experience the substructured reality of intimacy. Despite the modification to be seemingly illogical, for within nature encompasses all of intimacy, we must concede that it does not embrace the unity of intimacy within a subjective experience. Being a generality, it lacks a detailed account of what it encompasses and consequently cannot be considered an absolute unification.

Polyphonic Dialogue: Unity and Coherence

Monotheism also perceives the individual as a unified entity contained by an organized structure, appealing that thoughts are in context of other thoughts. Expending the psyche as a unified structure demands coherence for its thought structure, for within each pattern of thought postulates a direct lineage to other thoughts. When there is a sense that the specific strands are unwilling or uninformed to its relation, it appears to be incoherent. Coherency is the general appearance of thoughts, even as it cannot justify itself within the domain of the thoughts themselves, there is a sentiment that correlates with or esteems the unity of the system.

We encounter dialogue which has multiple exchanges employed at the same time, one which retains the aura of coherency, even though each detailed conversation does not connect to another. For this reason, it observes a sequential phase, sustaining multiple conversations recognizes the altogether unity by the ability of the participants to follow the trajectories. Even though the dialogue in linear form is not coherent, by the individual ability to form a coherent interpretation, develops itself to be coherent.

This is almost a game played by the participants, which tests the keenness towards a unifying mental capacity that can deal with multiple conduits without entrenching in a particular one. This can be accomplished by establishing themselves in the wholeness of their psyche, as if to be embedded in the coherency of the system, for whatever is brought by it can be handled. It becomes intriguing for listeners and readers to manage the direction of thought, which elicits an underlying sentiment of coherence stimulated by these intrusions.

Comparable to a combatant recruit who is stimulated by the training with varying tests of fitness in a temporal moment. With the various stresses upon them, it accentuates a unified experience. We cannot affirm a precise ability to measure out the definition of a combatant, for it encompasses not only the multiple abilities but a universal experience of an absolute unity for all warfare considerations. Expertise is not the imperative part of training, it is the existential experience accessed when tested from multiple angles, something that cannot be articulated or practiced.

This is comparable to parenthood, a multitude of intrusions for daily existing. What develops is a unified measure of the notion of parenthood, which has the ability to maintain coherence even as the complexity cannot be forecasted; by dealing with each particular aspect of the present moment. An absolute and finalized parent is one who can be coherent despite the fact of these intimate intrusions which test multiple fronts, all the while maintaining the ability to be removed from each of the particulars, alike the listener of polyphonic dialogue.

Therefore, coherence is not the concrete attachment between the strands of thought, rather is the recognition of such. We can entertain features of thought which do not endure a diatribe in a logical manner but still elicit a unified system of thoughts. Incoherence would become evident to provoke a conversation without the intentionality of continuity at any temporal moment. There must be some logical sequence that can be endeavored as a kind of unification; and when not the case, what results is a lack of coherency, in which each strand of thought cannot be connected to the rest — even as it always is.

Subjective and Objective Theory

The preliminary conception that the nature of a higher life form is an individualistic entity is essential for asserting that one's thought process is bound to the specific organism. The aspect of being preliminary is indispensable for understanding the implementation of monotheism. To experience selfhood, one would need to rely on a theory which does not correlate to anything related to selfhood. If we, as it were, reach into the box of selfhood and find a component which will produce the theory of selfhood, it will only be achieved from the vantage point of that element alone. The rest of the box is unwilling to share with a theory that arrived from within the individual, an attribute of an internal component. Similar to a junior employee who assumes the vision of the organization, despite their ingenuity, will be unheeded precisely because of its internal origin.

We must venture outside of the box of selfhood and find a theory of reality for a subsequent version of subjective experience, then we can implement the data. The mere attribute of externality from selfhood will enjoin the ostensible disparity between external theory and subjective selfhood. The limitation being that it will always be divided from true integration and will sit outside to whatever degree of analysis and integration. Through frustration, one may seek an internal version of it; however, when seeking such from within the box, it will be sensed as only an internal development, one which does not correlate to the rest of the system.

Conversely, for a polytheistic version, it will find an element in the box to construct reality and structured selfhood, disregarding the internal integration to that component. Its expenditure will be the particular element, e.g., vengeance, becoming the only manner in which to perceive experience, with a submissive resentment towards the possibility of a greater reality that has been outlawed.

While monotheism will always remain an external theory, one which cannot perform the absolute integration of the. That is the tendency for a monotheistic society to vacate to a key city or a foremost country for the attribute of serving as host of the leading culture. This activity must be done as a physical transition to fulfill the monotheism vulnerability. The completion of an individual integration of an external theory, one must reside in that communal locality to encounter bodily exposure to be experienced in its real sense. The communal body, especially the one that represents the theory, will be the nearest experience for something external to internally manifest.

The other measure for the embodiment of monotheism is to interact with an external element that is hoisted to represent the theory, especially when the interaction is related to the body. However, communal integration is a further embodiment than any personal activity as it is structurally factual to our senses. A common consequence when not alleviating this vulnerability is a lack of integration of the personal domain, or becoming misplaced in the theory itself to assume reality is experienced within its domain, disremembering that the theory is external. The resulting measure of the former is a fissured individuality and the latter, extremism.

Individuality as an Entity

Once the individual is established as an entity in their own right, we can observe systemic thoughts to be personal. Until then, each particular thought is as if reality has been enunciated, in which we can only perceive the information from a non-first-person position. Approximating a narrator which has been allocated from the vastness of the universe, which so happens to occur in one's mind. Moreso, we assume it to be the most accurate description of events. Reality and thought are not distinguished; being assumed the same will be the cause for much anger. The anger is due to a psyche that perceives its innate thoughts as the sole legitimate response to the perceived encounter.

Freud had termed this 'magical thinking', where the psyche is imbued with omnipresence embedded with an assumption of the power to change and influence every level of reality. At the root, we can find a person who does not distinguish themselves, for the reason that they do not contain a theory of unity or separation of any reality. In some sense, reality is observed as part of a continuum, instead of consisting of parts which make up a whole, it is a whole to whatever is being experienced at the moment. There is no notion that the experience is a central locality to perceive reality, rather takes the space of everything and anything. The fact that the neighbor experiences differently is not examined, for either they are mistaken, or it is the same mechanism in some manner of translation. The demarcation of individual experience arises from a theory, for the natural tendency to assume the experience to be the equivalent throughout the system; both internally and externally.

Wholesome Experience

We can readily justify the polytheistic view with its attempt at unifying the experience instead of a reality framework. The experience, according to the monotheistic view, is part of a larger system which does not prove itself to be insulated and deserving of cumbersome attention. When there is a Theos for *war*, the experience of *war* is unlike any other, making the individual become aware of the experience with sequestration from everything else. The experience seems deserving of its unique temporal location and is digestible for its full depth and vitality. While the monotheistic view approaches experience with a certain hesitation — for what brought it here and from where does it goes. In the attempt at unifying the experience, which is to say, indulge in the entirety of the experience, one will overlook the surrounding environment.

The experience itself is hailed as the only element that is deserving of a "monotheistic" notion and should be unilaterally unified. There is a dread that some existential information might be lost. In the example, the experience of *war* will appeal an apprehension for not being copiously engaged with it, consequently, it is safeguarded with an appropriate Theos. We can perceive this sentiment as the ultimate romantic notion, which will go further than all else in the romantic sense of the experience. However, we often find that such a mindset, of descending into the object of interest, or perhaps the wholeness of an experience, is met with a different outcome. One which is devoid of the fullness of any experience, contributed by a lost sense of self per a degeneration of its relating element for the object of interest.

This is because the theory of monotheism is factually correct and will make itself known in any endeavor. The experience is not endless and will become exhausted at an interval, considering a person does not have the capabilities to continuously handle the experience with further depth. The experience is rather a part of a larger picture, which if not attended, will cause the experience to substantially diminish. It is difficult to distinguish the true romantic from a polytheistic version, although all will become known in the outcome.

The Ambiguous nature of Monotheism

When we must pinpoint the nature of the material that is termed monotheism we are at a loss of articulation. That is because it is a theory of reality that includes its reflexive form within the theory, neglecting to distinguish a property other than the structure of reality. Yet, it must be sourced from some temporal position, which if we were to attempt further, would become a form of polytheism. Due to the disparity of having a localization for an aspect which seeks to decentralize, by attempting to access its source will cause the theory to reverse. However, we are required to relate to a central site for which we can articulate and detect. Besides, we must recognize the materiality of the source if we are to take the theory seriously.

The first theme can be accomplished by creating a version of the source according to the respective level of self-understanding. Like a mirror that reflects an enhanced version, this would be the 'best possible version' which we are able perceive for the *present* moment. When the reflection is not the paramount version, it will be relatable nonetheless but wouldn't be implemented into the entirety of selfhood; for there are psyche components that can perceive of something superior. Although it will remain relatable, for the attribute of portraying a version that transcends a relatable understanding, it will be removed from social affairs and will be wholly ineffective for the psyche. This is easier of the two themes, for we can readily formulate this.

The second theme correlates to the origin of the psychotherapy tradition and requires some discussion. Technically, a substantial theory should be capable of implantation without recognizing its source. However, because this theory is both partaking in the entire structure of reality and subjective selfhood, it will need an uninterrupted arrangement of animation to preserve its relevance. We require an address which we can attribute for the safekeeping of the theory; to ruminate the faculties of its research. When the relation to the source is lost, we don't sense an intellectual obligation to transmit its ideas. Not only does the source essentially need to be relatable, which can be accomplished by the aforementioned, but it needs to be intellectually articulated in tandem with the level of intellectuality of the particular psyche.

Potentiality of Monotheism

Every insightful strand of information that is contained in the communal library is reliant on its traditional transmission from its commencement. Intellectual material is no different than any organism which is dependent on its progenitors for longevity. The *potentiality* is always a part of its later materializations; when we sever that potential, a subsequent failure is suffered to all those dependencies. This has something to do with the lack of intellectual depth that was taken for consideration by those in the process of formulating modified intellectual material. The *potential* is the highest mode of profundity given to any specific piece of material that goes along its chain of transmission and advancement.

For illustration, if we were to detach the Hellenistic intellectuals from our intellectual community, we would find a subsequent degeneration in many unassuming advancements. Those which remain durable in such an investigation can be acknowledged to contain a contemporary *potentiality* which does not rely on Hellenistic predecessors. Such is the case for the psychoanalytic tradition, which contains enough *potentiality* that with a complete uncoupling of the Hellenistic material it would still preserve such scientific prowess. We would alternatively find the medical community to become a skeletal form of its present-day status. We can understand that whatever the medical material, it does not contain adequate *potentiality* to last on its own, especially because it is absent of a philosophical undertaking. We would find most of mathematics to substantiate its ground owed to the later infusions of *potentiality* by its prolific history. This might be the reason that mathematics and its branches have been highly effective in this contemporary era; for instance, computer science and physics. The philosophical material itself still seems brittle in the contemporary era. That is, we seemingly haven't found later infusions of *potentiality* that would exceed the Hellenistic material, thereby relying on them, even as being from an ancient world. Had philosophy continued with respective dynamism, we wouldn't necessitate to reach into the past for this dated *potential*.

Consequently, we need to identify the potentiality within the theory of monotheism so that it remains with its dynamism intact. This potentiality can be identified in the following manner, either by its source or from the notables or communal bodies which have infused a particular brand of *potentiality*. These can be found in societies and their luminaries which conserve embedded monotheistic tendencies. Undoubtedly, profound works of literature indicate notables that have saturated a certain degree of *potentiality* into the monotheistic idea. States which orient themselves in a manner that exemplifies the theory will be another instance. Philosophy and many other disciplines are another exhibition of the monotheistic notion. Thus, we will find many avenues of *potentiality* that will ensure a containment for the theory.

Threshold for Assessing a Relationship

The recognized threshold when assessing a relationship is a crucial moment of interaction. When done with exacting attachment it will result in a polytheistic version of the notion of monotheism. At the outset, assuming the interaction was erected with reliability, is free from constraint and unassuming to be the all-encompassing object of interaction. When the interaction is furthered beyond a certain point, it becomes a vacuum of experience. The object behaves as an isolated entity which is self-serving for the individual and whichever subsequent character. Then an elaborate portrayal of the object is envisioned, which so happens to be aligned with a projection of the underdeveloped aspect selfhood; externalizing personal deficiencies onto untapped potentialities. This object becomes a mediocre version of personhood, with all the assumed virtues and none of the vices; like an objectified relationship. The relation is not unilateral and is treated as unable to embrace a significant portion of the cumbersome experience, let alone the universality of existence. Thus, the object is presumed to be all-encompassing but is interacted as it were of such an inferior level for higher life form interaction.

For the psyche, the resulting theories are considered to be authored by something feeble as it will only affect elements of personhood that find the interaction stimulating and interesting. By way of example, the romantic encounter will be supposed with the same results. When it first unravels, it is believed to partake in all senses and subjective experiences. When prolonged without the availability to enchant the entirety of personhood, it falls from its ranks. The subsequent shallow experience is due to a portioned aspect of the psyche which is partaking in the affair. The romance, in some sense, has become local and devoid of all of that universal and communal flavor. However, it may be still treated with "monogamy" and expected to perform a futuristic development as a domestic couple, as if they were encompassing all of their experience. Especially the sexual performance, which makes use of the entirety of the body, biologically and mentally, which is being accomplished by a relationship that is only effectuating a partial component of the psyche; thereby, weakening the sexual drive with an assumption of an air of universality.

Analysis of Suitable Romance

The same interaction with the object that adds dynamism to the theory would also be the occasion of wearying its substructure. Similar to meeting one's idolized persona, which can either enhance the already enchanted version or would be the cause of a vertical moral decline based on those dissatisfied results. A relationship that hasn't engaged for an extended duration can be shaken to animation, alternatively, a relationship in perpetual continuity will terminate the animation for the ability of romance at any later date. To perform the relationship task appropriately, it must meet the same criteria as the romantic engagement. The location must be communal and cultural, the experience all-encompassing and poetic. The existential self must be available and willing for the engagement, and it must be meaningful to the moment.

More importantly, which is the struggle of all romance, the separation should be enacted at the appropriate interval which doesn't permit an overextension. The overextension phase will not only lose the potency of the romance, it will stretch the quality and cause a quantitative version to overwhelm the initial quality. Thus, the detachment of romance should be administered with a certain sincerity, although with the ability to prolong its memory in reoccurring cycles. That is the idea, when the departure is calculated, the romance will be alive in spirit while becoming an element of the bygone in its physical and structural sense. When uncalculated, the romance will be slightly afloat in structural terms and lost in spirit. *The moment remains a moment when it is treated as a moment.*

Uncoupling the Romance

The process for uncoupling is one of disremembering the moment, both intentionally and unintentionally, and to be revisited for ushering the spirit of the romance. Even the nostalgic re-visitation should be treated with veneration, as when overdone, will become a monotonous moment despite being highly animated at the time of its inception. The notion is that it should be utilized when there is a dry season, to apply its sentiment when it would be existentially appreciated by additional partialities of selfhood. When that application is no longer an interesting interaction, it would be discontinued for other tasks and interests. This is to ensure that the initial moment is both potent at its inception as well in its subsequent memory. Eventually, it will no longer be a satisfactory substance, and other notions of may be sought. The manner of uncoupling is also difficult to perform. For if it is done too rapidly, seemingly parting from the encounter, it emphasizes a lack of poetic sincerity. This would be unfeasible for the existential moment, becoming entangled with the existential self.

The subsequent objective after an absolute moment, compelled to continue its streak with an impending stretch of quality, is a distracting deviation. If that objective were too hasty there is a risk of transference from one party to another. This would be analogous to the aftermath of a romantic moment, if stimulated towards a tedious physical task, will not be experienced as a separation, for only psyche maintain the ability to distract towards the abyss.

While if the objective of deviation is intellectual, then it would become a disconcerting experience for the psyche, meshing two extremes which are in contention. This is comparable to a stern intellectual engagement that successively must apportion for an emotional engagement, a mediation that is untenable for the psyche. The middle ground is most suitable for separating from the romantic experience; modest, non-ritualized bodily tasks or unsophisticated intellectual engagement are best. The idea is that the objective should be uneventful for life to continue just so, to be considered a separation from normal grounds. When an eventful task is performed, it shadows or supplants the poetic moment, which threatens its legitimacy and continuity.

Monotheism as the Integrate for Relationships

Monotheism can also be seen as the relationship material of two correlative proponents. Through the prism of experience, we relate to the being, idea, or object. To relate, is to mirror a concept with one's experience, in which monotheism can be perceived as the mirror which performs the reflecting substance. To be able to reflect is another way of putting forward the ability to possess the nature of reflection for the object.

Whatever eminence the individual possesses, having an external aspect with the ability to be reflected against, allows selfhood to approximate experience. Without an externality which can reflect selfhood, it is fairly difficult to relate to oneself. A relationship is dependent on its ability to consistently relate from an observational viewpoint. The same applies to external relationships, which become more complex when there is a notion of relatability from a third-party perspective. Between two people, while each could relate to the other, it lacks a sensibility of relatedness which is demanded upon them. Much like one who doesn't contain a mirror, to relatively become less self-conscious in their manner of appearance. However, it is also the case that there is no demand upon the individual for any regard of their appearance. The mirror serves as the third-party arbitrator, making the critical demand, which either proves the result of a self-conscious person or a sophisticated level of appearance.

We wouldn't credit the mirror as the anchor for this growth, but we would recognize the necessity to establish a sense of direction. Thus, a relationship between two people, deprived of a third-party mirror for the creation of a demand, would have the experience and its relating material to lack direction. Each side of the relationship becomes cognizant of a watchful eye in the form of the natural connectedness between all of nature; including them. This is coupled with a recognition: this reflection of nature is aware of the full scope of the situation, comparable to the mirror to contrast one's realistic appearance.

Because it is an external theory about the structure of reality, it has the advantage of being aware as a third-party observer. The awareness does not require us to focus on the source of the theory, just as a mirror is inanimate but is quite obtrusive in its demand upon appearance. The demand arises within the individuals of the relationship, and the theory only serves to highlight both the individual's current state and potential as perceived by them.

Therefore, relationships are dependent on a third-party observer that serves as the external demand and recognition of the situation. The same applies to a relationship with oneself, which is dependent upon a third-party mirror. This comes in the form of one's childhood caregivers, which are the reflections that allow one to reflect upon themselves. The nature of reality is such that we can only relate when we experience an externality relating to us. The level of relational material which this externality engrosses is the degree to which we can relate to others. To build a relationship with oneself, one must appear to their identifiable personhood as if they are a third-party in observation, which would have the 'third-party perspective' relate to the first-person aspect of selfhood. When those reflections are not available or lack proper sophistication, all in accordance with the full extent of personhood and external reality, one must find reflections that are suitable for such a task. Thus, when other social beings prove to be an obstacle, the theory itself can be made use of. Corresponding to the case of using a mirror as an alternative to a friendly critique for the development of appearance.[5] This analogy also suggests that for two phenomena to be connected through monotheism, they must share a common source or essence.

Monotheism and Relationships

Monotheism and relationships are interconnected, the more monotheistic

---

[5] The psychological objective for a.i.

a society or individual becomes, the more associated and relatable is their orientation. When war societies become more prevalent, their social relationships develop to be less complex. When there is a principle such as a Theos for *music*, two dissimilar individuals cannot share in that relation; the Theos is seen as the vitality for the element of music, parting out the individual interaction and its relation. Nor could one communicate a musical relation with the Theos itself, as individuality cannot relate to a Theos as a source of vitality, for their presumed individualistic deficient vitality for that musical capacity.

To illustrate further, if one principles a Theos for *birth*, they could not relate to the elemental birthing aspect, seeing as the vitality of *birth* does not reside within them. Furthermore, they cannot relate to the Theos of *birth* because the entire vitality of *birth* is external to them. Nevertheless, polytheistic societies maintained relationships with deities, people, ideas, and things, as this was the natural response to reality and objective association. Polytheistic societies conserved those relationships as they sensed an intuition to the objective truth of the universe, something after the fact to be acknowledged with striking clarity.

We have before us two ways to perceive monotheism; one, the interconnectedness of nature and two, a relatable aspect for phenomenon. Ultimately this plays out in the two opposing fields of academic sciences, the sensual fields of study and the intellectual counterparts. The romantic fields engage in the relatable aspects of phenomena, while the intellectual department attends to the interconnectedness of that nature.

When we relate through mediums such as art, theater, poetry, and fiction, we are attracting external aspects for the purpose of connecting selfhood to its contents. The study in such fields is the realistic subjective experience of monotheism. Monotheism stipulates that indeed all things are connected, to now have the ability to be in relationship to anything. The connectedness of nature makes possible the sensual lifestyle.

The academic is busy adjoining objective reality with a modest disassociation of the personal experience for its premise. We require the academic to provide a landscape for which sensuality will extend and broaden relationships. For example, through science, we theorize gravity, whereas the sensual fields of study might interpret gravity in terms of personal experience, and thus issue relevancy to what the scientist unfolds. At the extremity of every scientific discovery will be what an individual might find to be socially relevant. The task of science is to unearth the possibility while the sensual department is to decide what to do with it.

The Existential Dread of Monotheism

In the ancient conviction, monotheism is perceived as a principle that correlates to a material entity, one that brings harmony to all thoughts and matter. The idea of believing in such interdependence would have been considered outlandish by the ancient psyche. When we could merely attribute phenomena to exacting sources, why take the existential leap and bind everything; hence we would need a notion of rationality to make use of rationality.

Let us consider that ancient society was at a prior stage of consciousness, a temporal locale such that when becoming *aware* of something new it would be assumed to contain a self-derived energy. Becoming self-aware is ambiguous, for instance, the element of music will comprise many levels of consciousness, to become aware of music affiliated with Beethoven is at a varying degree than former periods. The novelty of a new realm jurisdiction of consciousness would subjugate existing concepts, being that they are affiliated to prior formulations of selfhood which is likely to invoke an existential dread for their dismissal.

Hence, a distinct Theos becomes society's reaction to each stage of development, as was the case for the escalating Egyptian civilization. Even though consciousness is a persistent manifestation, there is the likelihood for epochs of drastic advances, one that would trigger a fissure of large portions of selfhood with its coinciding existential calamity. It seems that the ancient Egyptian civilization was an eon with deep and abiding concern with the problem of existence, developing a mythology that attempted to answer the questions that arose from this quandary. Ikram (2003) notes, "Ancient Egyptians believed that the afterlife was a continuation of earthly life, leading to a complex funerary religion including mummification, tomb building, and the use of funerary texts."[6]

A generation who excessively dreads about their existence can be regarded as allocating the burdensome nature of new information. As is the case for the digital age, overwhelmed by paralleled existential demands and dread. We can assume that such societies are becoming conscious of novel and outsized portions of their innate beings that are reflected by the expansion of the objective realm. With an array of this conciseness, questions in the form of existential instability arise, seeking relative solutions. Notion as to where they determine themselves to be contained and adequate in reference

---

[6] S. Ikram., *Death and Burial in Ancient Egypt*, 2003.

to a former state of reduced consciousness. The Egyptian endured a penetrating self-awareness to contrast the pre-dynasty era, which kept them searching for multitudes of Theos to attribute these aspects and to have existence travel alongside such progression. Comparable to the element of *music*, for which each level of consciousness requires a new understanding in its relation to the realm of existence and to the psyche.

For ancient Egypt, each novel awareness that leads to consciousness would mandate a new and diverse Theos. For instance, if they had achieved insight for *music* in its filled depth, something that prior existence had little consciousness of, they would assume that it contained an idiosyncratic force that bequeathed its dynamism. Because the contemporary manner of thinking is vastly different from the ancients, we may not realize that what we now accept as a fact was once an absurd principle. The idea of yesteryear is the reality of today.

While the idea of Theos as an existent entity is highly debated, what remains of monotheism is its features despite the notion of Theos as an entity to have been delineated. Monotheism brought society the notion that existence is of a single fabric and can be viewed in each of its parts – in that it is part of a whole entity. This distinction between principle and factual becomes significant when relating an ancient concept with our contemporary language. When we use the term monotheism in a contemporary conversation, we must note the ancient model from which these concepts stem.

When nature is interdependent, which can be considered an objectively true aspect, it will become available for reception as being *factual*. A picture of Hiroshima engulfed in a mushroom cloud with the caption "E = mc², " would self-assuredly note that rationality does relate to reality in the most tangible and horrific manner.[7] Unlike the presumed association between rationality and the destructive potential of science, this was rather a transparent conclusion that rationality is the deepest form of certainty and thus nature's interdependence doesn't necessitate more proof.

---

[7] Time Magazine Cover: Albert Einstein | July 1, 1946

Monotheism and Civilization

Civilizations and Theology

To understand how monotheism is operational between states, we must narrate for the exacting boundaries that formerly existed from state to state; not in territory alone rather in how the ancients regarded non-state constituents. They did not gain the impression that there was a shared individual likeness with those neighboring states. What occurred within their neighbors' domain did not disturb their respective understanding of reality. Analogous to one who is of intellectual supposition and expends time amongst an uneducated populace, even as they endure ridicule for their perception of reality it would not be to the detriment of that perspective. Understandably, there is a divisive route which does not allow other perceptions of reality to corroborate with their own. Besides the intellectual confidence in their respective studies, there is also an existential barrier between them, as if they don't share the same individual experience. Evidently, with a dosage of compassion, we could have anyone connect to another, indeed, this separation arises precisely because one does not seek to sympathize with the resulting alignment with them.

The circumstance in which neighboring states contained theological views that were contrary to the internal homogony of the state was of much indifference to the ancient world. Considering that theological propositions were theories of reality that took responsibility of most other viewpoints, the external populace were secluded as specimens of different origins and destinations, thereby not contradicting their reality framework. The sub-higher life form, such as the mammal, who witnesses a scenario would not be considered and adequate perception. The distinguished condition of Medieval Europe, for whatever reason, could not assert an existential distinction with constituents from one state or another. This may be owed to the Christian thesis on compassion, which overcame ancient boundaries and incorporated all higher life forms under a single unit. Of present-day, the Catholic Church's primary political aim is to view higher life form under a single unit, and to concern for it. With all higher life forms as a single criterion, boundaries are broken but so is the influence of ideas; especially ideas about the structure of reality.

Multiplicity of Theos and Boundaries of State

The principle for a multiplicity of Theos would be accentuating a lack of unifying matter in creative energy which parallels the framework of reality, allowing for the notion of division between states. This allows for the compartmentalization of life and personhood, for each experience or aspect does not require an agreement with another. One can entertain a reservoir of conflicting thoughts and not concern that they reside in a paradox, since external vitalities are of idiosyncratic service to them. The differing state is possible with an absolutely divergent orientation of reality because it is another animation of reality that does not need to be correlated on a principal dimension.

There is no single identity or self, and therefore, does not seek to experience the totality of life. Every major concept deserves to be positioned as it were, without interacting with other seemingly connected concepts. This holistic view would be established only within the concept itself so that it would be the comprehensiveness of the subject under investigation. To some degree, this is logical, for the contrary perspective of singularity would be seeking the entirety of perspective without the ability to attend to the various details with sufficient attention. When affirming all of nature to be a single thread, one will not find the wholeness of existence within the subcategories of specific aspects. They are only subservient to the interconnected state of affairs and will never be pledged to buttress an experience of their distinctive merit.

Psychologically, one may engage in a single fixation, essentially proclaiming that all aspects of personhood deserve to be employed in a singular idea or notion, all without parting any periphery for other mindsets. They do not want to let go of their fixation for they wish to experience that specific arena under high resolution. Analogous to a collective organization, in which each member does not experience the completeness of that collective. *Unity* and *peace* would not be a virtue for polytheism, since peace is the endeavoring to bind different elements.

The Setback of Monotheism between States

We have ample availability to claim that monotheism is a primary source for cultural conflicts. Since a society that is available to multiplicity would not be perturbed by neighboring Theos, let alone cultures or orientations of various existential aspects, monotheism positions as the thesis for cultural parting. This is an argument that permanently can be conveyed towards a monotheistic culture, in that the polytheistic culture privileges to offer that availability, indeed, with the coinciding detriment of the notion of unity or interconnectedness.

We may be unaware that contemporary determination for peace is the very fact that one precautions about the notion of peace, especially global peace. In a polytheistic society, they are not concerned about peace and tranquility, thereby *war* is not something they find troublesome. Only due to the monotheistic notion did the moral apprehension about conflicts yield its renowned effect. Thus, monotheism replaces the territorial dispute with a cultural one, which delineates the corporeal expense as its final consequence. The tension of this disparity will retain elasticity towards grandstanding against a dominant monotheistic culture.

Another point of consideration is that even as monotheism does have the adverse effect of cultural rivalry, consequently it is through monotheism that we are natively concerned about that trait. The notion of tension as a disturbing trait manifests only in a cultural space that seeks a measure of unity, and without it, there would be an indifference to discord.

One mode of thought that monotheism stands is the prevalence to rather concern with the profounder layers of existence than protect the intricacies of current knowledge. Even as war and its terrible effects are sensed, the monotheistic concern is not disturbed by it. It is more substantial to have a purview which demands a concern for all phenomena than a particular entrenching in a fruitful island amongst a biosphere of decay.

The idea is as follows, if a state would allow for a multiplicity of Theos and thus their neighboring cultures to be employed with no restriction, then it cannot embrace itself as a solitary entity. Although non-essential wars will be prevented, there will be no privatization of the state and no home territory to call its own. Even if one were to concern themselves with alleviating the possessive tension, they will not be able to retain that thesis for an extended period, having to regard whatever movement the wind blows. The only way to maintain a perpetual thesis is to maintain continuity under the political organization, which can only be accomplished by its unification.

Continuity and Unification

We are arriving at the intersection between continuity and unification. When something is unified it can endure, whereas what sustains onwards is consequently unified. The mere fact that all of history is founded around civilizations and not individuals or unified collectives is a validation for this premise. The unity that is characteristic of civilization contributes its supremacy to be prolonged in the future. If civilizations were to become subdivided, a deterioration will soon follow, whereas the unification of a state can allow each participating member with a certain allegiance to perpetuate it forward.

A prolific scientist who hasn't adapted to the contemporary methods of communication and conversation will have their research misplaced. The unification that surrounds these discourses is a pledge for that prolongation, with the substance to be preserved by the collective, provided that the collective remains unified. As a collective subdivides, the information that was recollected becomes scrambled.

What gets divided cannot thrive onward, for instance, foodstuff becomes subdivided into our metabolic systems and cannot thrive. Nevertheless, it becomes unified within our organic structure, which then metabolizes a partiality of the individual performance for ensuing endeavors. Those metabolized actions will either be a division, which will be a cessation to its extension or will be an amalgamation that will lead it further. Breaking a rock for the objective of building, at the instant of division, prevents the larger rock from actualizing itself as an entity. When the two portions are used to construct, the unification into a superior structure from a standing rock gives it a purposeful entity far exceeding its original state. How will the structure be used, how will it be maintained, and to what designation will animate in the conceptual realm? Those answers will determine how effective the support was for its final unification.

Polytheism and Monotheism in Egyptian Dynasties

A classic polytheistic society which reigned strong at its cultural height would be the Egyptian empire. This contradicts our previous notion that a subdivided society is in a state of decline. Indeed, those theological subdivisions are resolutely threatening the singular substructure which we call the Egyptian empire. The solution was to develop a reverence to their array of state ordained Theos-es; an ironic admiration that would have them intersect into the monotheistic notion, confined to a class-defined arena to bring about that unification. The elites of Egyptian culture would be able to participate in that harmony, while the majority of the populace will sustain that multiplicity.

This was not a polytheistic society, since the Pharaoh claimed a certain role of unifying the multiplicity of Theos, and thus brought a self-imposed monotheistic notion. The *king* had theologically and physically created the continuity of the ancient Egyptian empire, as such was glorified in life, and attempted immortalization in their death. This is how the populace perceived reality, but as the matter turns out, the reigning power was just honing the monotheistic idea, leaving the populace to be scattered into subdivisions. While the *king* appreciated a certain continuity in the orientation of reality, the lower echelons of the public had ordained the *king* with that experience, although entailing an orientation of a simplistic polytheistic society. Hence, we find alongside their culture an emphasis on the elites, for they gain the prerogative of relating to reality as it were, while the rest remained in archaic formation. This existential question hovered over ancient Egypt — if the interaction with the multiplicity of Theos can be accomplished, then should it not be fortified by something superior to a mortal?

Distribution and Bureaucracy

Distribution would be a regarded virtue in a polytheistic society as each element needs to be expressed as standalone. Bureaucracy is a manifestation of such, as each level of its organization is so detached that it would be difficult for it to take notice as a collective body. When experiencing its bureaucratic elements, one would gain a sense that there was no individual to represent the organization, seeming as if the collective appellation was sole element of preservation, without existing for its objectives.

Each member of a bureaucratic collective experiences the same disengagement, as there is no managerial associate to represent a unifying voice. Each individual within the organization is considered secluded in reference to relegating tasks, whilst also being a part of the collective to protect the collective posture. Essentially, the bureaucratic worker is to never seek innovation, all the while, defend the present ambiguous notion of the collective. The bureaucratic organization manifests like a scattered psyche, where there is no respite in the relationship due to the inconsistencies and lack of reliability. Everything is scattered into specific corners and when one illuminates a single corner, it does not further illuminate any other. No promise or futuristic ideal can be entertained since it would not be applicable to consider any aspect — a promise is a self-propagating notion which can meet at a future interval. The aspect which will grant the promise today will be neglected by the tally of the promise is to be fulfilled, whereas another aspect that is not connected to the promise takes its place. The constitution of such an organization is that it must distribute its tasks in a manner which remains disconnected from the hierarchy of power.[8]

They essentially loathe the interconnectedness for it reflects the

---

[8] (A forthcoming work will establish the significance of institutions, especially political institutions, *Institutional Structures*.)

democratic notion of government. In a democracy, the majority of the populace is the ruling class, which grounds a distribution of power. Each member contains a tiny fraction of that power, that every constituent can be titled a state on its own. A democratic society is constructed of multitudes of miniature states which all come together to form a society. These miniature states are persistently at odds with the main state as they are tasked with apportioning the power from the overarching state. There is never a resilient unity in a democracy because each member of the majority is taking power from the other. They are united in the agenda of dividing the power, one which will always lead to the diminishment of power.

Democracies have a stern expiration date owing to their inherent constitution for the division of the state. The hope is that the populace does not take the doctrine with too much earnestness, and rather borrows from the aristocratic/corporate or monarchical structure. The extreme democratic notion siphons the power from its innate existence.

The stern bureaucratic institution can be viewed as a powerless entity that has one job; to continue its continuity despite that. Each member has no right to power and cannot enact competent and proficient work. They are more destitute than the confined inhabitants as there is no determinate conscripter. There is no conspirator, as a democracy in its fundamentals would not want to retain a principle. More accurately, the majority of the populace, by stripping tiny increments of power away from the ruler or ruling class, have tied their own hands.

Monarchy and Interconnectedness

We may want to assert that a monarchy reflects the interconnectedness with its hold on power. There is no division amongst the populace, especially concerning matters of state. Therefore, a bureaucratic center within a monarchy will either be the most effective institution or the poorest, nonetheless, it will not be bureaucratic. The problem with a monarchy is its reliance on a single conscripter, who can rapidly move to either side of the pendulum. With unity, this is always the dread, which the masses, already unified, will fall prey to its sway. Or worse, it will gain notions of power for themselves to threaten the stability of the dominion.

Contrasting, within a monarchy, the household becomes a democracy since the unification of the regime transcends the borders of the private household. Each member of the household is unified with their neighbor with some degree of similarity. The ruling members of a household cannot exact sufficient oversight, since they are equally unified under the monarchy. The members of the homebody are ruled by their citizenship class and are equally regarded. This is the nature of life, we can be interconnected in one institution, to be divisive in personal affairs. The interconnectedness of the state results in the household being divisive and the divisiveness of the state produces the household to be interconnected.

Three levels of Institutions

This signifies the idea that monotheism and its interconnectedness, as a cosmic notion, is divisiveness within the governing body, which then produces dynamic reciprocity with the interconnectedness of the household. However, when there is a monotheistic notion in the governing body, then there is divisiveness in the cosmic and household realm. This is the motif of the homebody as the monotheistic attaché, which places that interconnectedness in the household while the state remains polytheistic. Monotheism when enacted in the household will compel the governing body to be democratic and divisive, which then causes the universal notion of reality, or the cosmic, to be interconnected.

Distribution in a Polytheistic Society

Distribution is meant as an antidote to the realistic nature of a binding potency with nature. Even in the polytheistic society, they must deal with the problematic insistence of a binding potency that evidently makes an appearance. We could not function in a strictly polytheistic society, for whom should take the role of oversight? With multiplicity, the components must attach to a single aspect, which cannot be relegated by binding all that multiplicity at once. Essentially, higher life forms must contend with their intrinsic unity in dealing with the perceived disparity among nature. Therefore, there must be someone who takes the role of a monotheistic Theos, who accordingly can convey unity to the differing energies. If there were no distribution put in place, the social environment would have their attachment to the Theos deteriorate, in return, they would wane their attachment to consciousness and awareness. We may wonder why this was not the natural manifestation of perceiving reality, for why polytheism was the standard in the ancient world.

Polytheism is mirroring the expansion of consciousness; as we cannot become conscious of all phenomena in a unified manner, those elements which ascend will be assumed to be unique in their source. One who becomes conscious of the experience of *parenthood* will not equalize that new insight with all other areas of personhood. Therefore, the natural tendency of a society that becomes conscious of profound aspects will attribute a precise

Theos for each of them.

The Commonality of Theos in Ancient Culture

When we follow Theos of any ancient culture, they all have in common that they are mirroring critical concepts of life, elements which they had more consciousness of. The revolution to take place in Egyptian society is to claim that those elements of evolved consciousness are interconnected by a single conscious continuum. There is no evidence for that interconnectedness, as each is understood as a self-contained and self-sufficient concept, thus the binding force has not been made aware of. Even as culture is acutely aware of the profundity of *birth* and *death*, they are not aware of the same profound manner for their interconnection to other aspects.

Contemporarily, our level of consciousness with regard to *birth* and *death* is greater than in how they connect. We are exposed to *birth* and *death* more perceptibly than we are to their connection. Initially, only through a principle which leads to rationality can the connection be made. Moreover, even the initial development was only obtained with a principle beyond the conceptualization of reality. When ancient culture found high levels of consciousness, such as the aspects of *life* and *death*, it was accessed through a level of conviction to an unknown arena.

Fundamentally, the progressive culture leads the conversation away from theology and into personal development. They are attempting to have the ancient culture become aware that their developments make use of an initial shaded conviction. A developing culture takes the further step by attempting to make use of that for individual experience. Ancient culture, as demonstrated by progressive culture, is uneasy about allowing interconnectedness to be a natural phenomenon. This is because they have taken a position upon the development sequence by being the arbitrator who can regulate that interconnectedness, in which higher life forms and the Theos are dependent. As the monotheistic culture advocates for the universality of the polytheistic position, the ancient stagnation had them repel that continuity because they want the role for themselves. This catches polytheism in a bind because they claim to be the theologian who will seek out the true state of reality but, when such a reality is offered and thus threatens their position, they entrench themselves. This demonstrates that it wasn't philosophy that motivated the intellectual aversion to monotheism but rather was a form of pride.

The Objective of Civilization

The abstract concept that gives rise to the civilized structure is placed upon a chain of reactions which emanate from a center towards its outer receptors. Since it is abstract by nature, it would only involve a theoretical framework that attempts to breach the physical structure which has the final outcome actualized. When abstraction attempts to fulfill an orientation of individuals in a given structure, it is built against higher-life-form likeness, a form that is not privy to an abstract makeup. In so far as there is a method which preserves civilization to be the complete theory of abstraction, it will prosper, whereas the ensuing populace undertakes ideas which don't align with the wholeness of the theory, it will begin to unravel and become uncivilized.

Civilization parallels the homebody, which offers a reflection for its constituents residing in the structure, reminding them of their distinctive developments. The home has another function, placing a physical structure and organization to surround the abstract notions of psyche ruminations. Without the home, whatever the conscious gains, will be unheeded by the organism for the fact that there is no biological manifestation of them. Therefore, we have two primary elements at the root of civilization; one, to remind oneself of what is existent, offering a reflective image, and two, a biological manifestation of abstraction.

The first of the two is bound to the perpetual interaction between personhood and the structure. Comparable to how guests of a home will not enjoy an adequate reflection of the home structure when mistreated by the homebody. Despite remaining undeveloped in certain subtle ways, the primary impression will be in reference to aspects of neglect. The same holds true for revisiting one's domestication after an extent of disengagement, to fail to serve as a locality to elicit a sentiment of concern for an adequate representation of themselves.

The second of the two can be a vital force even after long epochs of disconnect between theory and locality, just as the home which has been deserted can remain a locale to offer a representation of the ideas of the constituents. This would be proven when the public becomes interested in a persona to revisit their former localities. They are looking for a representation of the person despite the extensive interval between their interactions with these localities.

A city would be of the same material, which even after there is an abandonment of its foundational theories, will be a representation of them for a long time to come. Thus, we may be unaware of when Rome had lost its connection to its theoretical foundation, but we can be sure that it was many centuries preceding its physical demise. The same can be said for any civilization, city, state, or country. Therefore, we may be interacting with an environment, being only a representation of itself, just as we would interact with a home and assume to be connecting to its hosts.

There will always be a lag between the representation and the person or theory, considering that the home or city is not really an abstraction but only a representation of it. When there is an expiry between the home or civilization and its hosts, the interaction with the representation will automatically lose the absolute experience of the theory. Similar to the person of regard to which we visit their prior localities to gain insight and interaction with them. There is a separation between them and the locality, and our interaction would not necessarily be sufficient to gain an embodied experience of the person. However, had we interacted with their home when they were still hosting, we would have been able to gain an embodied version which could be considered near absolute.

The greater the gap between the representation and the host, the less embodied the interaction becomes, representing minimal improvement in uncovering the developed theory. The keynote for identifying this phenomenon is by recognizing if the city is "alive," which is the common phrase of cities claiming to "never sleep." The phrase is only of use to deduce if indeed the city is alive, in which we experience the city as would a home that has the host nearby, and not as a home that feels uninhabited.

The same applies to global civilization, or global influence, in which at each moment there is only one city which is the source of the theory's influence, and the rest are to be representations of it. We will acknowledge this through many factors, but most often by the experience of the city to be absolute or deficient. This requires an aptitude of subtly to be able to identify the real thing versus the representation. For those lacking this depth, we would find that a common thread amongst cities in which they point to another city in all of its marketing.

The application of the constitution or theory to an existing city or homebody which lacks the vitality of present representation is a complex inquiry. This would be based on a unique relationship with that locality, one which is consistent of the complexities of a proper relationship. Yet, even with a degree of a perfected relationship with the locality, it still would require an intellectual base in the form of a theory. Since all relational depth requires a breadth of knowledge and intuition, this would be the ultimate source of all these localities. The relational aspect is the conduit to produce the desired effect, while the intellectual material is the source of it.[9]

Subjects as the Container of Civilization

Not all intellectual material is consistently equal for this effect: we can first relinquish substance that cannot be applied to a practical lifestyle. Second, we can forget the theories which are not in response to the needs of a generation, thereby requiring that they must be in dialogue with the present communal conversation. Third, it must not override prior intellectual depth and must be a mode which only furthers the already formulated intellectual strides. We can go on and on, which will eventually lead us to a theory of reality which is consistent with the depth of prior theories and the present existential state.

All intellectual material has a sort of aspect that can be interpreted as a theory of reality. Mathematics would represent numbers, which are multiplicity and intervals of time. Therefore, it would be fair to say that mathematics is a theory that states that reality can be divided and pinpointed. This would signify in practical terms that whatever enters perception can be recognized in a certain form or point, and that reality is deserving of that complexity. However, mathematics does not account for that reality in direct relation, and only through many layers of analysis can we arrive at a theory of reality.

The student of mathematics will not follow that sequence thoroughly, which has the ultimate theories to remain dormant in their subconscious. Each discipline can be of a similar effect, while we would find certain subjects to be in closer relation to that theory. For instance, we can find the disciplines that naturally reach the political scope to be more parallel in reaching that marker. Psychology, philosophy, social sciences, political sciences, and gender studies are all close to that theory, so that within its domain is the source of civilization.

The political aspect endows it with its relevance, not for the objective nearness to the ultimate theory but as a pathway towards it. We cannot place the theory from an objective point of conjecture, since the communal dialogue and their interests are the means towards that conversation. The formula is such, for political proximity as one metric and objective-subjective proximity as the other.

The theories that are most perfected may not emanate from the particular locality that is sourced for global influence. In fact, they intersect, so that besides political proximity, to be intersecting with the city of primary

---

[9] (To be further developed in a forthcoming work, *Representations and Reflection.*)

influence. This may venture further to be the intersection of a particular component of the city, however, the system halts at the city's gates, and identifying a specific nook to be the source is a redundant inquiry. We could say that the fact that there was a lack of intersection between the city and the theory had caused the theory to lose its political veracity. This is a more complex dynamic, for what is the basis of this interaction?

We could understand this by way of an adjacent idea, which is that political relevance is always found in the city and incremental dosages outside of it. Therefore, the political relevance of a theory is partially tied with the city of influence, which if not for it, would be answering a dialogue while being outside of the existential conversation. We could post the communal dialogue to any part of the world, however, to interact with the dialogue in a dynamic fashion would require existential and psychical participation.[10]

---

[10] (To be further developed in a forthcoming work, *Elements of Civilization.*)

Consciousness

The Development of Self-Awareness

Another way of distinguishing monotheism is through the ascent towards advanced consciousness, whereas pathology is the digression to concentrated levels of consciousness. In this context, consciousness is the awareness of selfhood and its varying components, while pathology is the digression to retain the animation of particular components.

Intuitively, we must declare that the advancement from mammal to higher life form was primarily an accomplishment of consciousness. With that degree of self-derived awareness, we are able to dictate and control the organic system with the psyche apparatus. This heightened level of self-awareness enables us to influence and govern the organism through the realm of the psyche, suggesting that consciousness plays an essential role in our ability to regulate the system.

Indeed, self-awareness may have emerged through introspection of innate personhood by its relative experiences, accessed through humility, in which we recognize our absolute state in tandem with reality; implying the reflection on one's innate nature is vital for developing self-awareness. The concept posits that humility is the pathway to achieving self-awareness, wherein acknowledgment of our accurate nature aligns with the coexisting reality.

This is the best orientation for a sub-life-form specimen to obtain; that is, if we were to create an ethical system for them. With a variability of humility, they will manifest an inclination to observe the state of affairs, with the eventual context supposes a dearth of a wide-ranging exploration. Prior to every stride in comprehension is a less acknowledged facet of accepting the possibility of that very understanding.

For illustration, a mammal may aspire to a higher level of consciousness in whatever level of consciousness they already maintain at present moment. This process would involve recognizing its limited knowledge, admitting its gradation within the realm of nature. Through that awareness of a realistic state, advanced awareness can be born. In our current state of contemporary form, consciousness has expanded to levels of self-awareness which comprise an expansive landscape of experience and phenomenon.

This amelioration of contemporary awareness is owed to the circumstance of certain conditions. When we neglect systems of thought, we lose the resulting awareness, relegating those notions to the subconscious. The first stage of decline is when the subject of investigation loses awareness of itself. This is the process of transitioning exposed concepts from the conscious backbone to the subconscious helm. We can perceive existence as a state of awareness in which its bottommost form contains a strand of subconsciousness. The plant, for instance, contains a slight state of subconsciousness.

Subconsciousness, by its definition, lacks innate self-awareness. Without conscious intervention, the subconscious has great difficulty in obtaining awareness of itself. Higher life forms ingest forms of nature that comprise reduced forms of sophistication, so we must assume that the material of ingestion contains a substrate form of subconsciousness. This is because we have only gained consciousness from elementary subconscious states, whereas we evidently do not observe a reduced form as we repopulate the general organism. Consciousness arises from a subconscious realm; thus, all of nature can be considered a form of subconsciousness.

Consciousness, Subconsciousness, and Nonconsciousness

To proclaim that consciousness arose based on its innate development does not do justice to the psychological research which taught us the relation between the conscious and subconscious. The subconscious must have ascended from someplace; we could either stipulate a similar form such as the 'nonconsciousness' which initiated its provision, or tolerate the notion that subconsciousness never ceases to exist in all phenomena. We can posit that by being unacquainted with 'unconsciousness' in the field of science it must not exist. The problem is that subconsciousness, by its definition, lacks the ability to be aware of itself, more so, to be able to evidently articulate that. If subconsciousness sprouted from some preliminary shape, we must find that organism which embodies that liminal state; one which hosts the acceleration towards a subconscious state.

We would all agree that mammals are embedded with a subconscious form of sorts, which also allows concurrent higher-life-form consciousness to sprout. Which organism can we find that develops from 'nonconsciousness' to subconsciousness? What characteristic is it embedded with? We may find that subconsciousness never departs but only loses more awareness of itself, just as the subconscious realm contains some awareness of itself. We can perceive its skeletal substrate in our intuition even as we cannot articulate it.

Instead, there may be this 'nonconsciousness' which can evolve into subconscious form. Then the inquiry becomes — is there a form of awareness at the atomic level?

With psychological tools such as analysis, we are able to use active and particular consciousness to bring forth what has been submerged in the subconscious realm. Some material would never have been conscious while others could be actively repressed with the assistance of the conscious realm which is encrusted upon the subconscious. Another conscious individual, possibly the clinical professional, can bring awareness of the subconscious material that is dormant within the patient. The clinician's consciousness is subsisting in the patient's subconscious to become self-conscious. Similarly, the patient could use their distinct conscious psyche to find the subconscious layers and become aware of them. The point is such that we require an element of consciousness to elevate the subconscious to a higher domain. Arguably, this can be applied the other way, where only consciousness can dispel other consciousness, whereas never being threatened by reduced forms of consciousness or subconsciousness.

In a similar vein, we could train an animal to perform tasks beyond their instincts by employing our conscious guidance. While the mammalian brain is primarily subconscious, it can be brought to a certain level of consciousness. Theoretically, even a plant can express itself beyond its natural state devoid of external chemicals. In the plant's case, a layer of subconsciousness might harbor the potential for a heightened degree of consciousness. The process of evolution from plants to higher life form can be seen as a profound shift from the thinnest layer of subconsciousness to the absolute higher-life-form consciousness.

Even higher-life-form consciousness encompasses disparity amongst populations, with some individuals far more aware than others; e.g., the child and adult. Since the plant's consciousness is fairly limited, elevating its subconsciousness to a higher degree of consciousness would be a challenging objective to replicate.

A higher-life-form subconscious realm that manifests can be viewed as a disremembered or repressed form of consciousness. This perspective leads us to deduce that all phenomena were situated in an antecedent state of consciousness. Theoretically speaking, the advancement of higher-life-form consciousness makes it more available to awaken consciousness to all of nature. Just as the dog trainer conducts the dog to perform a measure in contour with higher-life-form socialization, conveying consciousness to the dog, so does the competent social being warrant consciousness to the plant.

Monotheism in association with Consciousness

An exposed element, to which we describe a notion or degree of nuanced selfhood in reference to itself, or otherwise the surrounding environment, is the initiation to consciousness. Despite its reluctance for change within the system, it enlarges a perspective, which through reflection denounces an organismic structure and adheres to its gateway of power. The power for which it would be anachronistic towards deficient sensibility for the ability of motion granted in containing the aspects of absoluteness. Under the rubric of the exposed element lies its contained material, with scrutiny will enable a second persona which handles the regulation system of the first. Consciousness thus becomes: the intermediary between naturalistic evolution and a division of space to ignore, subvert, corrupt, or enlarge the system. Working in that regard, with its concerning entity beyond nature as perceived henceforth, the intermediary separates realism from absolute realism; for monotheism to produce an external theory that undertakes the mechanism for us. The difference is the mode of interaction, as to approach this sensibility either through theory or through exposed selfhood, no matter the origin.

We can acknowledge this when we learn of a reduced experience of consciousness during a disengagement from communal interaction. The exposition of it, through any measure of means, will not be accomplished had the detachment taken place. Much can be said about the communal; in this regard, it is not only theory that is held in the base of these foundations which transpires consciousness. Only that the communal contains the embodied monotheistic activity, in the form of the limitlessness of reality in terms of the exposed dynamic relationships. With that degree of assumed reality to be demonstrated for all of our senses, allows the theoretical framework to become absolute. The communal performs such a demonstration and allows the free-flowing sentiment to run unabated, to which the adherer will benefit with the capability to enlarge and maintain consciousness. Such is wilted when lost to the evidential production of its absoluteness, which consciousness, although not theory, will be maintained within the associated protection which the theory offers as well in its own domain of self-derived experience.

We have for ourselves a bilateral arrangement; without both participation, each will begin its peculiar stumble towards its intrinsic vice. Consciousness, however it arises, would include an element owed to the capability of stating this notion. Such capabilities do not stay their ground, for the entire environment is opposed to seemingly extensive ability for control in any department. The decay of it comes without its maintenance, and thus theory which grants a security of abstraction, disallowing that mortality will come to its defense.

While more can be said for a theory which does not interact or expound on the physical manifestations of reality, consciousness at the helm, although contrary to the concrete physicality, serves as an indissoluble connection to its system. It can be above absolute organisms to interact with the abstraction which theory is a part of, while being intrinsically tied to its predecessor of absolute physical function. When we reflect in the territory of monotheism, it does not contain the capability to interact with organic material, being of pure conceptualization. It finds solace to contain a strand of material which can serve the divide, as consciousness is pleased to perform that function. In some sense, if consciousness can be abstracted to theory, it would pronounce a theory of reality similar to monotheism. When monotheism is sought for its physical manifestation, it would be formulated as a form of consciousness.

Preoccupation with Forms of Thought

When one is preoccupied over certain forms of thought, they neglect and forget other thoughts. For instance, a pathological compulsion may result in losing awareness of thoughts unrelated to the compulsive line of thinking. While one is excessively focused on a particular body part, they will disconnect their conscious mindfulness from other parts. Let us venture to say that the reproductive organ is the body part that higher life forms are indeed most cognizant of, accordingly, there are more conscious associations with that organ than others. We are constantly fluctuating in and out of awareness towards components of personhood and the objective world. While one is more conscious of their body, another would be of their mental dialogue, and a third in their relation to the social environment. When a focus is transfixed to certain rigid parameters, they in their wholeness become the transfixed material itself; thereby, losing attachment to the rest of their psyche, including that which was civilized and developed through advancement.

Concentration of consciousness not only serves as an information gateway to the entirety of personhood but also stands as the ultimate recipient of that information. In this context, attention material is synonymous with the psyche. Granted we always would be engaged with specific material, although the fluidity of refocusing to another domain will compensate for the slight fissures of personhood in that redeployed attention. Within that fluidity is enough relatability between the attention material and the new material which would labor to create a fusion of the information. When we multiply that material throughout the psyche, we possess the capacity to identify a certain selfhood which becomes the observer of attention. However, this is technically not accurate since the only concrete form of selfhood is the material of attention. However, with a high level of relatability between strands of material, we would consider them to be in tight association with each other. So much is this intertwining that it would be considered to be the same unit.

When the material is experienced with a lack of relatability to each other, there would be a strong formation of selfhood, as the relationship has become quite pathological. There is no transparency for the connection between attention materials, fused with the same stamina as biological connections. Instead of the psyche becoming a habitat of disarray it becomes a fusion of all the information without space or fluidity between them. They become a singularity because of the fact that there is no relatable information between them, in other terms, a highly masculine form of assumptions, presuppositions, and pathological focus. In adding a biological component to the array of the higher life form structure, it will coalesce because it doesn't contain a degree of differentiation between them or substantial relatable material.

A Loss of Relationship Material

A perplexing thing about the nature of the psyche, (and to indicate to the scientist to identify such in the rest of nature), is that devoid of relationship material, it will interfuse and not remain distinct entities. Given only that there is close proximity between them, for instance, an individual's house will be an assumed biological part of their form unless relationship material maintains them to be separate and interacting. The same would be applicable for family, work, country, state, city, and objects. The only requirement for the object to become synthesized with the psyche is that to remains adjacent and additionally, that it doesn't become a part of a relationship dynamic. It would be fairly difficult to justify the senseless neighboring state without a relationship notion, yet it may be that it has dissolved over a gradation of time, and for now, to be an assumed bas biological part. We can identify this to be one of the primary causes of problematic dealings with family, home, work, state, and objects.

For those lacking relatability to the attention material, a sense of self would be at the primary objective of the psyche as there are limited details that could create disparity throughout the thought process. In a certain sense this is biologically correct, a result of the organism as an entity apart from the rest of experience. Comparable to how an underdeveloped couple evolves to become similar; not being dynamically engaged; the only method of connection defaults to blend as a biological singularity deprived of material between them; *codependency*.

Where material is engaged contained by a relationship would not manifest as a singularity, as would an absolute romance. Indeed, there is a certain compensation for the romantic behavior which would entail disregarding the pseudo-relationship material: as is the case for absolute romance which would steer away from anything related to technicalities and other non-potent material. Instead of the psyche being tasked with the attention material of a vast array of trivialities, it is treated with only a couple of highly potent pieces of information. There is a stronger form of fluidity between them which costs the psyche with a reduction in ego-formulation or a sense of compound unity. However, as is with absolute romance, the identity of the couple is slightly lacking but compensates for by being highly relevant to the occasion. This would be the same result for the psyche, in which the formation of self is also a fluid state but when called into the material — becomes deeply engaged.

Pathology is Natural

Coherence as Biological

There is a natural mobility of interaction between thought-material, to which each thought ascends only while being associated with a prior thought. Arguably, it is impossible for material to emerge without circumstantial material that serves as the progenitor to its contents. Additionally, there is a sublayer of the psyche which solely serves as a cohesive element between thoughts, distinguished from the happenstances of normal activity. This is categorized as meta-material of the psyche that demands a sequence of formation towards any contextual thinking; as it adheres to its unique structure. The normal mode of mental material retains sequential properties, adhering to the data of the biological reality and dependent on an array of plasmatic connections. Hitherto, we anthropomorphized the psyche for conscious interaction and the field of psychology, we must remember that the theory must flourish under a biological rubric.

Supplementary to the inquiries of neuroscience which will agree to the sequence, coherence is the path of connectivity of plasmic connection. A field that will resist linking biological connectivity to coherence, consisting of this meta-material. For this aspect we must enter a new conceptual realm, in which the thought-material is absolutely biological and experienced coherence is a derivative of biological coherence or is one in the same. We may be unable to identify the coherence in the physical structure, for thoughts which are used for such scientific investigation is part of the requirement for coherence. Comparable to a scientific investigation which examines the existence of the observer who is performing the observation; it is redundant to a cyclical degree and cannot offer any intuition by its logical design.[11]

Consequently, there must be a rational continuum between thoughts, adhering to the rules of uninterrupted continuity. Rationality as the term insinuates, a 'ration' allocated to thoughts as they seek attentiveness. The thoughts that remain within the potentiality of the psyche, which in all likelihood will not manifest, are also a part of the rational picture. The subconscious thoughts and 'potential' subconscious thoughts can only be existent in terms of the coherent plasticity of the psyche. We would necessitate to dismiss from potential thoughts those which cannot be formulated with coherent continuity. For instance, we cannot consider haphazardly amongst the potential of thought to include a thought about a historic moment. We are under the specific social environment for which such content wound not emerge and there is no possibility to have our psyche facilitate such connections to consider such thoughts.

Making use of our imaginative capabilities we can immerse ourselves into a pseudo-environment of that sort, facilitating the emergence of those thoughts. While the imaginative realm can inform, it will not tolerate a recording of the intricacies of an imaginative picture, as would a perception for instance. The method for which the psyche uses par imagination to mirror perceptual pictures lacks the necessary sophistication to truly immerse oneself into the existential experience.

However, imagination is making use of perceptual data and ontologically would be fairly similar to perception. Therefore, the 'potentiality of thought' cannot consider perceptual manipulation which dutifully can place us in any environment by making use of the external environment via perception. The psyche at any given moment contains the potentiality of thought which is solely based on its innate system and cannot consider perceptive-related patterns of thought.

A future scenario is an illustration of the entire availability of the psyche, to which future exactibility is its limits. While portraying the most elaborate description, it is utilizing the present system and assumes its content to be aligned with the expected picture. The moment a perceptive-related picture interacts with the psyche, there is no probability that it has contained that exact information prior to the motion. We may want to consider that 'potentiality of perception' will attach itself to the database of potential thoughts. However, that would be akin to proposing that the innate potential is based on another external potential, for which even with the ingenuity of

---

[11] "What is certain is that complex cognitive operations are possible without the help of language." Laplane, D., 1992. *Thought and language.* Behavioral Neurology.

the imaginative capabilities, it cannot fathom such a scheme.

Perceptive Material

The position at the physiological helm of the psyche is the domain of perception and its imaginative heir. These remain above the psyche by its power to invoke thoughts which cannot even be considered in the potentiality of thought and are brought to the forefront of consciousness. This grants perception a bountiful amount of power, being versatile to the ever-changing external stimuli to be exposed to oneself. Removed from perception, within the strict framework of psyche, such thinking would not be considered, let alone attended with complete attention. Through the powerful mode of perception, the psyche and its happenings will be altered to account for the invasive information. Perception is no different than brain surgery which enters the psyche and manipulates its structure and system, differing only by the method of its intrusion. This natural intruder places us into immediate conflict between the subjective domain and the external influence.

We are bound to the statute of the psyche of 'fluid sequence', yet we must interact with our perception capabilities; inevitably obstructing that flow. The mode of perception does not account for the on goings of the psyche, essentially layering its specific information right on top of it. This can be considered like a second track on the psyche's project of thought and remains in that disparity throughout psychological life. The 'second track' becomes a form of pathology because of its inherent nature, disjointing from the stream of thoughts. Simply rejecting pathology becomes extreme, in which we demand to sever contact from perception itself. Perception naturally occurs, by way of our senses in their normal attention to surroundings. To keep in position of antagonizing the unnatural intrusion of perception, it would demand not only mental but physical isolation from the external realm. Such is the approach of the Zen tradition amongst others, who were not satisfied with natural pathology which occurs through environmental and social engagements. However, for social functionality, we must allow some notions of pathology.

Pathology at Intervals

In reality, we must pathologize at intervals, since complete adherence to rationality and coherence must report for all thoughts and their corresponding levels of profundity. We cannot welcome complete cohesion unless each component of the psyche is allowed natural expression, each according to its profundity. When we attend to the sole thoughts of the present moment, we must treat them as a complete cohesion of our own. When we do not allow each pattern of thought to be recognized for its own sake, as expected we neglect the proficiency of information material within that domain of thought, becoming non-actualized thought patterns. For instance, if we were meditating about infantile stages of our development, a reflection which did not allow the thoughts to be profusely experienced, notwithstanding for the purpose of maintaining a rational psyche of adultness, we would be neglecting the intricacies of those patterns of thought. Essentially, the pursuit of rationality can be the cause of a fairly incoherent system which passages past thoughts that necessitate a higher degree of attention and attunement.

Therefore, we must enact secluded thoughts as subdomains that would entail rationality that follow their distinctive parameters and do not necessitate rational networks to the overarching psyche. Right away we can reflect the parallels with identity as a rational subdomain that is not rationally connected to the wholesome rationality of the psyche. In whatever manner we postulate it, identity will not be cohesive to the full rational picture, for there is no rational reason to have identity interact with the wholeness of selfhood. The reasons stipulated amongst all the identities are attempts at mending that disparity, although fundamentally fruitless since the reasons are rooted in the identity and not derivatives of the wholesome rational picture. They will attempt cohesion within the subdomain itself, while exact cohesion is relative to the entirety of the psyche, devoid of a particular bias towards a subdomain.

Similar to the fact that perception-information is not rationally linked to the inner domain of the psyche, and by nature is treated as a subdomain from the totality of the psyche. Perception can be symbolic of the fact that cohesion cannot be solely meted out at from the top vantage and instead must be distributed as varying cohesive bubbles within a complete rational cohesion. The contradiction is such, having wholesome rationally to propose its cohesion for the whole lot while having the bubbles of minuscule rational structures with the leverage of not requiring mending with the entirety of the psyche. The rule of nature is a perpetual reproduction of itself throughout the network; whatever is acted out at full scale must be scalable and distributed throughout the system. Therefore, we are a single organism and trillions of organisms. The single organism is enacted at each level of sophistication so that we can identify ourselves as trillions of organic organizations or a unified entity encompassing its parts.

Pathology Deviates

These subdomains are pathologized and treated as the whole body, even as they are only a part, to establish access to all the information that is contained within it. Which raises the question as to the deficiency of psychological pathology, if it is a natural manner to sequester material and excessively fixate upon its substance despite the larger domain. We can approach this in two directions, firstly, it is not the indulgence that is the cause of pathological behavior but, rather the lack of attentiveness to the higher mode of rationality beyond a subdomain. The fixation occurs as a manifestation of the neglect to attend to the larger cohesive substructure of selfhood.

The second way to conceptualize the deviation is when indulgence itself is sought with further consideration than the principle itself, for being involved in the cohesion of selfhood. They are misguiding the pathological domain as the meta-domain of personhood, wherein no other realm necessitates to be recognized and developed. The attachment to the dogma manifests as a result of adhering to rationality with complete consistency, so that they may be considered exceedingly rational. This may seem counterintuitive as they are acting in a manner that would be perceived as irrational and non-cohesive. However, the directive towards such indulgence is accomplished by perceiving cohesion to be the only state of reality, especially the reality that has been presumed. They will not entertain any notion that neglects complete rationality, thereby, not allowing to entertain a higher domain, one which would entail an admittance of a lack of cohesion.

We can further understand this by the accompanying aspect of control that is quite prevalent in pathological behavior. *Control* is a perspective that the element of cohesion must be held together at a high expense. The notion of control is another way of viewing over-rationality, which seeks to perpetually administer cohesion throughout the domain from which they reside. They cannot fathom a disparity in thoughts, or within their principles, since doing such would altogether dismiss rationality. *Control* is not a psychological condition but rather a philosophical misunderstanding of nature. They do not understand that nature is rational and irrational — rationality contained by domains and meta-domains — and irrationality in the connection between subdomains. Perception, imagination, and identity will never obtain cohesion within selfhood, and we can be assured that many other subdomains exist that will be unable to form cohesive attachment.

We find another community of individuals who assert rationality as a method to not attend to the many subdomains, claiming that such interaction is not cohesive within the domain of the psyche. What occurs is that they incessantly reach up into the profundity of thought and become distant from their attachment to reality. The neglect of the subdomains, by the mere nature of their irrational connection, will be a manner in dealing with all non-rational subdomains. Starting with perception, which will wane over time with the assertion that rationality is comprehensive throughout the network.

Perceptual connections will dampen the realistic nature of the objective realm and especially the social environment. Thus, the parallel between the populace asserting rationality throughout the network corresponds to their social unavailability. They are unwilling to distribute rationality as a scalable system, and they must retreat to the inner chambers of the psyche, devoid of all of these "influences" which would deter perfect rationality. This may cause them to be altogether detached from reality, using their rationality to construct systems of thought that are unnecessary or destructive to the progressive realm, society, or sociality. With enough maintenance of the proposition, they will deviate from cognitive norms, resulting in the inability to use their body and speech in a coherent manner.

Ego, Perception, and Pathology

Concerning this, let's consider how the ego interacts with perception. Freud postulated that the ego is molded through perception, "Out of the welter of sensations which is poured into the ego, one group stands out sharply defined and of especial importance—the perceptions. They, as it were, mark the frontiers of the ego; it is at these points that the ego is prolonged into perceptual consciousness."[12] We are furthering this by stating that the demands of perception give rise to the ego at the outset, expanding Freud's view that perception gives the ego its form. The formulation of a voice of selfhood, the ego, is the contention at being differentiated from the perceptual realm. The attentiveness that one has taken in connection to perception is the degree of divisiveness to the internal structure, which is mediated by the posture of the ego to serve that division. We could say that without perceptual interactions, there would be no form of selfhood, nor would there be the superego. The notion of selfhood is a creation from the perceptual realm, just as a person born on an island will not experience the notion of aloneness. In our language and discourse, it can be understood that pathology is the seed in the creation of the ego.

Pathological domains within the subjective experience would correlate to one's attachment to their ego. The ego is the mitigation of perception and internality, acting the appointed position from the perceptual realm for the internality of selfhood. The ego's essential nature is in the allocation of the disparity in the system of thought, and when there is less disparity there is a weaker ego. The ego is the actor who embodies the middle ground between two cohesive domains, to ensure that both are not disregarded by their inherent contradiction. Those who adhere and prioritize perceptual

---

[12] This quote is from Sigmund Freud's *The Ego and the Id*, 1923.

information will be creating a more potent and formidable ego.

With all domains of pathology, the ego will be positioned as the *self* in concern for the mitigation of the two opposing domains. Therefore, there will be many egos which can result in them being contradictory to each other. The primary ego which was built by the perceptual disparity may be in contention with another ego which is serving a counter position in its particular mitigation. Therefore, the tempering of egos is necessary as well, whose task is to handle the disparity of the things that are dealing with their distinctive disparities. The superego is thus born.

The superego takes the tone of one's caregivers because the manifestation of the superior parent is setting the regulation which supersedes other guidelines, such as the ego's judicial power. The child can attend to their intrinsic judicial importance, but the superior parent adjudicates the finality of the child's regulation with a wholesome package. The ego has judicial power to mitigate the two opposing domains, yet the superego has supreme judicial power to mitigate two opposing egos. The superego can discipline the ego in any manner it sees fit; to promote more important mitigation to occur other than the ego's mediocre dilemma. The superego can place the ego into the realm of oblivion, or it could highlight the ego's dread with supreme judicial power.

The power of the superego is derived from the amount of ego-disparity in the system, which in turn, is the amount of pathological domains. The overburdening superego or varying egos are symptoms of a highly pathologized mental network. This may seem like a deficiency, yet, conceding to the fact that the superego and egos are responsible for the developmental success of the higher life form. The one who has removed pathology from the mental apparatus will not enjoy a strong notion of selfhood, and further, will not have an overarching superego demanding the individual towards progress. Just as a child who is not parented with an administering mode will not experience existential exuberance and will not feel the need to progress or develop. The administering of parents causes the child to be more pathologized but will also develop the ego and superego.

The difference between a normative superego and an ego is when the pathological domains pertain to significant notions of existential importance. For example, when the pathological domain concerns one's sexual tendency it necessitates to be mitigated by a pathological domain which does not view the expression to be *good*. The ego flanked by them will be mitigating these domains and reconciliation may not lead to normative success. The superego created from this ego can be owed to the disparity of the ego with an embodied ego for the perceptual data. This would entail the judicial power over the amount of allowance of sexual contradictions to be experienced in the perceptual arena. The superego's attention is being used for the judicial review of sexual inconsistencies relative to social environments, leading at best to restrained sexual interactions.

Considering a case that would highlight normative success would be religious identity that was pathologized. The ego is created to mitigate true selfhood from the identity, and a superego may be formulated to judicially mitigate this particular ego with the ego that is tasked with perceptual information. This would have the superego decide when it is appropriate to make use of the identity in the perceptual arena, or when to make use of true selfhood despite the perceptual arena. This can lead to a high degree of normative success due to the superego's insistence on regulating different aspects of selfhood in tandem with the social environment.

The Process of the Ego and Perception

We can stay aligned with Freud and the sexual factor that contributed to one's earliest state when engaging with perception. As reproductive vitality begins to blossom, perception becomes the vehicle for that expression. Sexuality creates distance from internality and externality, thus forming the basis for the ego. There is a love triangle between the ego, perception, and sexuality, in which each is dependent. With a decline in a representative voice of selfhood, sexuality becomes weakened, as there is no self to reproduce. Simultaneously, withdrawing from the consciousness of perception will lead to a decline in both the ego and the vitality of sexuality. There is no mark between internality and externality, thereby removing the need for a voice of selfhood. Additionally, there is no distinct individual to engage in its distinctive replication.

The ego arrives through the mode of perception even as it contradicts the cohesive flow of thought. With the modest attendance towards perception, we are breaching the continuum of internal thought with a new influx of housing information. A gap will always occur; designated as *track one* and *track two* with no correlation between the information of perception and the psyche's stream of thoughts. Perception becomes a form of pathology, even more potent than pathological behavior itself. Perception lacks a subconscious layer that connects the two tracks because external experience is not a dialogue but instead a recipient of information that has a dialogical imprint for ego formation. Studying and analyzing any pathological behavior could reveal subconscious connections as rationality is the network for all thoughts. There are subconscious subtexts that when understood in a coherent context would otherwise be deemed insanity. Insanity, even with the mumble of some incoherent passages, would, with enough analysis, be able to identify the stream of thought material that led to these words, making it a coherent sequence. This does not occur with the information associated with perception, as a complete intrusion upon the psyche, thereby without any rational connection.

Social engagements as an example; even as they are experienced through perception, occur as a continuation of the psyche's thoughts with the ongoing social dynamic. The thoughts between those two domains are aligned to the intricacies of the dynamic, making the social interaction something that transcends perception. The social dynamic becomes a rational continuation of internal dialogue. We may be able to find the subconscious subtext in the dynamic which explains the purpose of their social engagement, resembling a relationship expert treating two parties as a unified entity for they assume an intimate relationship exhibits cohesive rationality amongst them. However, this may hold true for less intimate relationships, as there is less investment from both parties, resulting in a lack of repressed subconscious material between them. The intimacy binds the dynamic where we assume the interactions to be habitually based on a continuing dialogue. Intimate partners do not intrude upon each other's subjective internal dialogue as strangers do, as they are not actively engaging in perceiving each other. Intimacy compels a connection of each proponent's internal dialogue and creates the dynamic to correspond the likeness of an individual to be studied as resembling a singular psyche. On these outlines, Freud articulates, "Every sexual act is a process involving four persons." He expands on the individual likeness of a dynamic, which becomes the embodiment of the two distinct parties and two more integrated versions. The social dynamic only appears to be touching on the continuing conversation about the dynamic. Therefore, we can rationally connect each interaction with its corresponding dialogue, without the dynamic ever becoming an external intrusion.

We could understand the psyche as the regulator of perceptual data, thereby we may assume that perception doesn't intrude but rather is subjectively measured. Seemingly, if one would take a look at a chair, the sight itself is compelled upon the psyche. Yet, the psyche builds configurations in preparation for perception, so that the details of the chair are based on preconceived notions ruminating the psyche. This would counter our proposition that perception imposes upon the psyche, as the psyche contains preconceived material that overrides perception. Still, the sight itself, the experience itself, is an intrusion upon the psyche. Even with all the preparation to frame the perception, the chair came about in a manner that is disconnected from the sequence of thoughts.

Preconceptions and Perception

At this juncture, we are reminded of the significance of constructing adequate frames to perceive the external realm. Encompassing initial constitutions lightens the burden of pathology for the system, as the external realm does not intrude on the psyche, instead, it is invited. Without clear frames to approach a perception, the entire experience of perception becomes pathological. On the other hand, with coherent and relevant frames to approach a perception, albeit the initial exposure being pathological, the concurring details will not be.

For illustration, the one who explores the concept of *chairs* with a degree of depth, will perceive the chair in congruence with that concept. Frameworks do not do justice to the fact that perception intrudes on the psyche. The preconceived concept of *chairs* becomes the foreground to experience the perception, however, the perception of the chair is detached, retaining information that supersedes those configurations. Take for instance the phenomenon of trance-induced recall or hypnosis that reveals details, material undetected during normal perception. The frameworks which were in use at the time of perception did not capture all the information and various details made their way into the psyche. For instance, consider a person who experiences a hypnotic trance to recall specific details about a past event. While in a trance, they vividly remember minute aspects, for instance, the intricate patterns on a seashell or the scent of a particular flower, material that was initially deemed unimportant to those frames. Nevertheless, one would desire to condense thoughts from perception with ongoing internal thoughts. This can be done by thoroughly studying the connection between perception and thoughts by means of finding subconscious subtext which unite; perhaps in the supernatural realm. This allows a superior awareness of reality or perceived reality to mend the perceptual experiences alongside internal dialogue.

For illustration, a common perspective may be; "Fate brought us together," "I was just thinking of you," or "There is a reason that we met."

This pattern of thought can be followed more thoroughly, "I thought about someone so they must need my help," "I ended up here because that is where I am supposed to be," or "I am seeing this because it relates to some personal matter."

We can find comfort in not overindulging in extreme thought patterns by recognizing a distinct separation between selfhood and externality. Even as *fate brought us together*, we will not further this axiom by saying that *fate demands us to never depart from each other*. The demarcation of two distinct beings cannot be overridden by any metaphysical perspective. Blurring the distinction between selfhood and externality opens the door for too many distresses. We can still attempt to enjoin in a transcendent narrative, something that cannot be rationally formulated but would answer the interconnectedness of perception and thoughts. For example, one perceives external happenings to conclude that they are personally relevant. Surely, this can have an adverse effect and lead to a variety of pathological patterns since we are making claims upon a reality without a rationale.

Faith can be a helpful instrument in reaching the territory that is beyond reason, such as our inquiry for making a composite of perception and internal dialogue. Reason cannot mend such a divide while irrational frameworks can serve as the bridge. For example, if we assert the notion that *fate brought us together,* all for the sake of connecting perception to internal dialogue, it would not be considered pathological. In attendance there remains availability for conjectures, for no rational argument dwells in that domain, conversely, when we begin to dispel clear rationality to enforce such a claim, it can become pathological. In essence, fate assists in mending the missing points, while rationality represents the points themselves. When either rationality attempts to mend more than it is capable of, or an irrational framework attempts to take rational precedence, it becomes pathological. When we do not mend the missing points, a circumstance arises with contention between two tracks of thought, formulating the foreground for pathology.

The Creation of the Ego

Imagine an individual attending to internal dialogue, suddenly, their perception is interrupted by a nearby conversation and its contents. This perception of disturbance creates a gap, a rupture in the person's ongoing stream of thoughts. Within this fissure lies the need for a bridge to connect the contending states, such that the person engages in a process of interpretation. However, integrating the disruptive perception and preexisting thought patterns requires the presence of a third-party identity, a mediator of sorts. The ego takes the role of the external intrusion to facilitate the integration of the two; in this context, the ego becomes an integral construct, playing a vital role in the interpretation and integration of contending states. Without the ego as a mediator between perception and thought, the gap between the two would persist. Consequently, the gap itself can only be maintained by a component of the mental apparatus which impartial to the natural flow of thoughts. The gap itself creates the ego, which is partially disconnected from selfhood so that it can contain this external information.

We can find the correlation between perception, ego, and pathology in the *seclusion* traditions. The leaders are simultaneously seeking to negate the ego while also isolating themselves from the perception apparatus. We find both the ego and perception are interconnected and if one wants to negate one, they must negate both. We may not be able to identify the characteristic which the *seclusion* tradition is most seeking, whether it's negating the illusory self, being less deceptive, or seeking isolation in its many forms. We do know that these three crucial components, elements that are characteristic of a *seclusion* tradition, are enough to assume their interconnectedness. The doctrines will wish to isolate themselves from pathology, even seeking to remove any external information that would give rise to pathological thinking, only to desire an experience with selfhood in its natural state. Thus, three concepts are interconnected, ego, perception, and pathology, in which each allows the other to be formulated and expressed.

Resolution for Pathology

A thought that lacks a coherent relationship to the context of inner dialogue or that of external perception can be considered pathological. In seeking proper succession of thoughts we must ask, what allows this thought to arise if neither experience nor context brought it to the surface? Through investigation, we will find that the thought manifests itself from the *power of the rogue state*. Previously, we have stated that the creation of the ego is what gives the rogue state its energy, which serves as an identity within an identity. The psyche is simulating the psyche, allowing another 'figure' to reside which is not bound by the guidelines of selfhood. In any case, that unified pathological entity takes control of the cohesive development of thinking. This is similar to external dialogue where one imposes an idea beyond the context of the conversation.

The immediate occurrences within inner dialogue become a primary locale in which all other contents of the psyche are subservient. As external perception is accented despite the events of the psyche, so too the occurrences of the psyche are the internal perception against the backdrop of all other thoughts. To illustrate, when one is jogging, all other body parts become subservient to the legs, even as the body comprises more vital organs. The experience of an individual's existing moment becomes the limelight of relevancy, and the legs take the role as the vital organ. When engaging in social conversation, even if the content is justly unimportant, it remains worthy of attention due to its perceptual experience.

This becomes one of the causes behind pathological methods, as we may choose to denounce perceptual content for more significant endeavors. However, the psyche does not perceive that transmission; during the perceptual data in this case the run, the legs become the most imperative part of the body. Despite this, without engaging in pathological behavior one can reframe the experience with something significant for personhood. This can be accomplished by leveraging the context of the experience to engage in more relevant associations. For instance, one may be engaging in a routine conversation about weather, as the forecast is being described they can associate to reflect one's conceptual preparations for the upcoming season. With these associations, the modest conversation becomes relevant.

Relational Levels

Pre-Scientific Philosophy

There is a common supposition that the realm of science and philosophy were initially a single study which fragmented into divisive disciplines, to even be considered in disagreement. We must examine and elaborate the instance which had them intertwined to then find their subsequent versions throughout the fissure. We will approach a single subject for the purpose of detailing the aspects that will help understand the lineage of knowledge.

An inquiry into the cosmos during the pre-scientific age would have been in reference to the lunar and solar cycles. Preparing a mathematical equation that would note the phases of variation would determine a fairly specific understanding of the systematic process of the two primary elements of the earthly sky.

This would not provide a sense of intelligibility in regard to the substructure of the sun and moon, nor to the energy which allocates this cycle, or the explanations for this particular path and its subsequent transitions. They would not understand the manner in which individuals are able to interact with the solar and lunar influence that manifests for Earth. Furthermore, we wouldn't gain insight into the reasons behind the subjective interest that circulates the mind in affection to the cosmic bodies which equates to other inquiries.

The only article gained from the mathematical inquiry is the established rules of transitions and their repetition. The slight deviations that are not noticed within the transition, for instance, when the moon appears the same but has indeed undergone extensive change, would not be available nor of interest. We can only explain the notion of time according to its appearance. Social interest launches beyond these parameters of research when there is a comprehension of calculated time and its attribute of change which is not in reference to the moon as a planet. The effect unto which the moon has upon higher life forms, or the sun in its varying seasons, would be the primary interest. Achieving insight into how or why would not assist in personal affairs, for how would the navigation of a vessel benefit from such comprehension.

Additionally, prior to a precise method for time, there could not be an interest in the calculation of time for these cycles. When the day or year is not divided into capsules of specific parameters, we cannot even entertain the notion of a certain cycle of the moon or sun. We would be aware that some varying cycle is in effect, just as there would be an acknowledgment of day and night. However, the specificity of those details would not be available until there is an abstract conceptualization of time and its mathematical associations.

The Advent of a Scientific Discipline

The reason for dividing the day into specific parameters is to style the day with a more nuanced understanding. With the day as a lump sum, it would not be accessible in its particulars. Above and beyond the morning, afternoon, and night, the day would be a general construct without gradation to its variation. Through dividing the day, we can access the fragments as if they are a 'day' in themselves; by such methods gain a more comprehensive access to the day.

This does not mean that we somehow gained absolute accessibility to the day as even the fragments contain possible divisions. Additionally, by focusing on the minuscule divisions we depart from the unity of the day and lose apprehension of its entirety. We could imagine dividing the day into further subdivisions which would be impractical to the experience of personhood. A capsule of time must be relevant to individual interaction and a millisecond is not a part of that equation. Personhood is not available to partake in such a nuanced measure of experience and rather is limited to what is represented in the units of classic time. Thus, we identify social interaction and relativity as the basis for the scale of divisions in time.

While there is a construct titled the millisecond, it does not belong to an inquiry of the pre-scientific era. There is a limit to the division pertaining to the cohesiveness of the entity of the unit. When we over-divide, the unity of the unit loses its recognition. Thus, we cannot comprehend a millisecond within the cohesiveness of the day. We wouldn't be able to approach the day through the lens of milliseconds. The number of divisions of the day would induce a redirection of our approach from the recognition of the day as a consequence of taking a minuscule measure of time. The same applies to the millisecond, which during its inquiry would become frustrating to apply to the day as a whole.

The millisecond is solely applied to social interaction when there is so much nuanced experience, requiring a further division of time or measurement, e.g., flashbacks. However, those moments that require milliseconds are so animated that even their encompassing day, month, and year are deserving of a new construct.

The Social Relation to a Scientific Discipline

We have surmised time constructs in a general sense, which by its social availability of interaction becomes time as we know it. However, each person has the ability and the availability to construct time in proportion to the importance of their experience. Just as we've identified the day, month, and year as significant quantities of time, we can recognize one's experience to be deserving of a recognition similar to the construct of the day, month, and year; even by way of bearing a collection of short moments. The cycle will continue just as in any other time construct, and those moments which converted into months, repeat itself in regular intervals alike to months and repeat their cycle throughout the year.

Thereby, if a moment converts into a *day*, there is a consequential *night* upon approach. As well, there would be a *month* that would surround that *day*. To determine the relation between the *moment/day* and its encompassing *month*, we would calculate the moment's real time, which in this case was determined to be an absolute day, and multiply by thirty. To perceive the moment in terms of an absolute day, we would need to rely on intuitive prediction of the relation between what an exposure of a regular day would correspond to, and contrast to that tier of depth. Sometimes, one must skip the measurement of the day as the moment may be eligible to be contrasted to a month or even a year; such is surely configurations of trauma.

Thus, the *month* completes itself only an hour after the moment, and a *year*; the next day. A *lifetime* would incur within two or three months from the initial moment and will subsequently lose its animation and become an irrelevant conceptualization.

This is the case when the moment is converted to a *day*, however, moments can translate to *years* which can be finalized within an absolute month. The ability for the moment to continue indefinitely is in the commitment to its conceptualization, or more precisely of the dynamism of the conceptualization in reference to the level of exposure to the psyche. This can be revived despite becoming greater than the conceptualization of a lifetime; no different than the medical community reviving a patient. Alternatively, by neglect, it can remain stagnant in time.

Therefore, there is both the universal and the individual sense of time and they can contradict or oppose each other in certain circumstances. The significance between these two aspects relates to the degree of commitment of the conceptualization, or in other words, the depth of experience which is understood by the individual; to be dialectical of either universal time or personal experience.

We apply the construct of lunar and solar cycles to personal experience, distinguishing it from only being a conceptualization of time. The normal setting of a person is in parallel with the experienced constructs of time. If a higher life form had taken a more sudden interest in their experience or if they had lost interest, the constructs as we know them would be altered. With a distance to experience, the day and week will not be parameters worthy of interest. While, if there is more proximity to experience, the minutes may be too long to encompass the nuanced movements of life.

However, the equations of complete cycles are universal and beyond the conceptualization of time. There would always be a certain cycle of seven and thirty since they are the rhythm of reverberation of an initial starting point. When an event begins, it will reverberate at the seven and thirty marks. Yet, we are not bound to the parameters which are between the spaces of each stage. So, there can be seven within each stage towards seven, or thirty within each stage towards thirty. The reason that we are bound to cycles of seven and thirty and not twenty-four or three-sixty-five is because of individualistic nature.

Seven is the *short cycle* and thirty is the *long cycle*. We would always necessitate a cycle which is far beyond the normal stretch. The number seven is fair enough of a separation to term it such, but not too much to be considered the long stretch. The number thirty is extended enough to be considered the long stretch but short enough to be relatable. We cannot discuss a year without being nostalgic and romanticizing the memory with imagination. The month can be discussed from a more realistic perspective, having a bounded scope of information to formulate an intelligible inference.

Anything less than seven is too close to an initial experience and would require some sort of separation for such an overview. We cannot refer to the 400th day prior which has a certain regard, although we can refer to a given week suffice that it's in the near term. Instead, to refer to an eventful day we depend on the construct of the thirty mark to fulfil it. While for the reference of a prior week, we depend on that same thirty-day construct.

When the duration of time is prolonged, then we cannot refer to the thirty mark and depend on the construct of the year. Thus, to refer to a day in a month is dependent on the year, which could not be referenced devoid of that. The day is not enough in its intrinsic nature to be an applicable reference point. In general, we do not refer to even three days prior without invoking the week. This proves its lack of validity in performing as a representation of a short span of time. On the contrast, a span of a week proves to be formidable in its application to memory. We could reflect back eight weeks ago, and still, it would remain versatile in social discourse. It begins meeting its limits beyond ten, which would require reference to the long-term construct of the month. The month on the other hand, is available to be referred throughout the entire of the year.

Once the year's duration is up, the reflexive edge of memory becomes faded. The construct of the year is somewhat ironic, in that one could reflect to certain years although would lose a logical continuum of the actuality of the occurrences. Too often it happens that one perceives years that were considered good and then takes a different narrative. This is because it lacks the materiality of substance, and we rely on intuitions and narratives to portray that particular frame of reference. While we could not convince one who is reflecting on the previous day or month that their experience was a certain character, yet for entire years or decades we could simply offer an entirely new perspective.

This discussion of time is not normal scientific discourse but would be a typical inquiry of the pre-scientific era. They would consider this alongside understanding the reasons for the particular cycles of time. Besides the aforementioned effects of the lunar and solar cycles for higher life forms, we can gain a relevant discipline by understanding the numerical significance of the particular cycles of nature. This would assist in understanding our experience of time. Thus, the inquiry into the lunar and solar cycles was additionally to understand how one experiences themselves relative to time and cycles.

This is the pre-scientific version of psychology, by using the disciplines at hand to further understand their own experience. Therefore, it came alongside philosophy, as they approached the already obtained study of the cycles with their specific intentions and context of gaining particular self-understanding from it. This opened the floodgates for limitless inquiry into lunar and solar cycles as methods for personal understanding. There was no need for relevance in pertaining to navigation to further one's understanding of cycles and their numerical significance, because they maintain relevant context of how we interact with cycles and the inner cycles within one's apparatus.

The allowance for limitless inquiry into the lunar or solar system can either be for two reasons: there is a pathway towards applicable aspects within nature or to use the knowledge as a method to conceptualize higher-life-form experience. The former would be the inquiry into the sun's makeup for the applicable measure to replicate and reflect on the objective realm, for instance, to understand the nature of fire and heat in reference to understanding fire-related properties. We could inquire to understand the elements that make up the sun so as to control those same elements on Earth.

The common thread is to use the sun as a locale of inquiry for which can then be related to things that are relative to us. There is no direct relationship, thereby, the sun would be in second-relation to the application. The inquiry into the solar cycle to achieve the division of time upon Earth is a direct relation. We relate to the time divisions of the sun and do not require an intermediary relation. However, when we seek second-relational applications, the sun becomes a by-product of understanding.

The Intricacy of Multiple Relational Levels, Pre-and-Post Scientific Era

In truth, our inquiry into time, both of the subjective experience and its historical precedent is exemplified using a 'direct-relational' conceptualization with the objective of conceptualizing another notion. Just as the philosophical inquiry of a time-cycle was done in the interest of understanding the experience of personhood; the scientific development of time uses a direct-relational conceptualization for second-relation experience. Technically, the scientist does not require the conception of the sun to investigate the elements within its domain, however, to research the elements would require a domain of inquiry which would always formalize its research as second-relation.

We may choose to use the elements themselves, e.g., hydrogen, for examination, thus bypassing non-relevant distractions. This will provide an outcome of the same results; the elements must stand in a position to which the inquirer must deal with them. A common scientific relational theme is the pursuit of reality in its most absolute sense, with the subject as a part of that wholesome picture. There is a disturbance when justifying the submission of effort towards a single element when we must existentially place ourselves in the composite picture as the objective. Thus, another relational juncture makes headway, although possibly unbeknownst to the examiner. There may be a certain excitement from the elements which are not found in the rest of nature. This sentiment can be narrowed to a particular pattern of thought to which they are related to a specific memory or experience; which would have the investigator captivated by a singular memory for the advancement of most of their efforts. We would wonder as to the seeming disregard for supplementary memories that may be compelling and deserving of equal attention.

The reason the scientist had chosen the *sun* for their research is because it remains relevant as a 'direct relation' to higher-life-form interests such as the aforementioned construct of time-cycles. One could find other by-products of relatable interest towards the sun yet becomes informal in the event of an available 'direct relation'. Comparable to the philosopher, through subjective and native experience could have studied the experience of higher life forms, making for an ancient psychoanalyst; however, they mostly reached into an already reliable 'second-relation' for the assistance of their inquiry. This would grant them more access to the particulars of personhood experience that do not get submerged when we approach too meticulously as would a psychoanalyst.

Thus, the difference between a philosopher and psychoanalysis is that the former uses second-relation for their inquiry, while the latter inquires in direct relation to it. The scientist, differing from the philosopher, is inquiring about the same second-relation but does not have personhood experience as its end goal but other aspects. The scientist is always in third-relation to whatever they are studying, first-relation is the subject, second is the elements of particular interest, and third, the relation for personhood. This can become extensive, with many relations, for instance, the sun, elements, chemical processes, production, and then consumption. This would be fifth-relation from inquiry until individual relation. The philosopher is arguably only titled such because they are always adamant to remain in second-relation, avoiding to either be in third or direct relation (psychology). They want to avoid the confusion of proximity that the psychology field regularly experiences and also the irrelevance to individual relatability which the scientific field grapples with.

When we establish a contemporary inquiry into the sun's substructure and its interaction with other celestial bodies, we can do so from a variety of vantage points. First, there would be a direct relation, which would include the yearly cycle, seasons, sunlight, daytime, and others. These do not necessitate to be explained with any intermediary conceptualization other than the normal relation between sun and individual experience. For instance, the sun is directly related to the sunlight exposure of an organism.

We can study sunlight to understand its components, inquiring about something that is in direct relation to ourselves. When the inquiry becomes too extensive, we find ourselves in territory that cannot be justified as a direct relationship to personal experience, becoming secondary. For instance, obtaining the measurement of sunlight would not be apparent as a clear relationship to personhood. How can personhood be directly related to an understanding of the measurement of sunlight? The measurement can be used in certain scenarios to determine the degree of sunlight for a design project, however, the intentional examination of the measurement prior to the application cannot be in direct relationship to that. Had the project commenced, and a measurement of sunlight was sought out for some direct relationship, obtaining that material is in direct relationship to the project, while second to the experience of the final construction.

Since we must create a scenario for which the discipline can be applied, it becomes an intermediary bridge for that relationship. Even something simplistic such as understanding the distinguishing factors of infrared, visible, and ultraviolet rays, it wouldn't be explicit if that was in direct relationship to personhood. Why would a person concern for the properties of these rays?

When we explain the specific scenario, possibly a concern of overexposure due to ultraviolet rays, we can find a relational property. However, since the general state of relativity is not directly interested in ultraviolet rays as would sunlight itself, the social environment requires some sort of explanation for the interest. Notice that we don't require an explanation for higher-life-forms being interested in sunlight itself. By being directly related, we don't require a medium between information and personhood.

Subjects and its Conformance to the Entity of Research

The rationale for an individual of ancient orientation to study these cosmic cycles would refer to the divisions of time or a solar/lunar influence which differs from that. We discussed that the division of time can be extracted from lunar or solar cycles, now we will investigate external influences that are assisted by mathematical equations of its cycles. For instance, navigation at sea would be developed according to a precise understanding of the lunar cycle. The divisions of the lunar cycle culminate in a comprehension of its cyclical nature that does not serve the divisions themselves, for there is no interest in the month of earthy change, instead researching certain stages before they arrive. Thus, the division of the lunar cycle for navigation is the ability to identify its subsequent stages for the benefit or consequences for which each interval offers. In essence, navigation seeks to turn every purposeful stage of the lunar cycle into a distinctive entity. The inquiry is to seek out the divisive components for their own sake, e.g., full-moon, and the navigator won't be troubled by a lack of cohesiveness in accordance with the full cycle.

The captain of a ship does not care for the lunar cycle as an entity but for the full moon, half-moon, and other celestial events which can infer a wholesome navigation. The only reason that there is any interest in the complete cycle is by identifying the stages at the expiration or commencement of those intervals, whereas the moon as a construct is not an interest. Navigation and agriculture, subjects esteemed for lunar research, do not investigate intervals of the lunar cycle which do not appear in the sky. Whatever is identifiable as a consequential interval would be the furthest that it would be examined.

Whereas the researcher who adventures the moon as a celestial construct would be concentrating on the intervals, areas of research that are not seeming in the sky or consequential for individual flourishing. They are questing the moon as an entity through its subdivisions, and for this reason, a more comprehensive understanding of the moon that grants access is appreciated. However, as we said there is a limit to those divisions, or complexity of detail, causing a reflexive desertion of the moon as an entity, to foster the focus of those details and defeating the purpose of the inquiry. If we wanted to understand the month as a whole by considering its subsequent days, we would not be furthering our indulgences through subdividing the month into supplementary divisions. We would start to deviate from the moon as a construct and identify another sub-entity that can embrace the division of those details that were attracted. Accordingly, if we divide the month into hours we would depart from the month as a method to encompass hourly intervals.

The Manner of Interaction with Society

The individual interacts with society by two coinciding elements, firstly, the interaction with the foremost theories which are the substructure of the communal system, accompanying are the relational interactions with the communal body. As we discussed, philosophy will always take the residence of 'second-relationship' and will become the arena which formulates all other theories and subsequent relationships. In response to its immediacy of relational level, it allows the prerogative of oversight of less intimate interactions.

If we build an institution, the constitution of the institution can be considered in second-relationship to individual experience. Primary is the vision which partakes in the institution, and second is the interaction with the institution. Any subsequent developments from the institution will be 3rd, 4th, 5th, or 6th in relation to individual experience. The entire institution rests upon the secondary-relationship of its constitution. A direct relationship between individual experience and the institution is never possible since we must understand the instigating material that has the individual interact with the institution; differing from the family structure, one which does not require a mediator to justify the interaction owed to the biological connection.

Accordingly, philosophy becomes the underlying theory of a societal conceptualization or a communal body which distributes itself throughout the system with varying degrees of subsequent relationships. We could always study, for instance, a tradition and find its underlying philosophy, and through that inquiry, we can recreate the tradition in our respective systems. The tradition is a communal body, and by connecting to its culture through a variety of mediums, will interrelate with the overall philosophy from varying degrees of relationship.[13]

For illustration, the flag of a country will have varying degrees of relation to the experience of personhood. The flag and its art form foremost, the representation of the art form in an interactive formulation, e.g., 'fifty stars under one state'. Then it is extracted for a philosophy of 'unity through division' which then can be related to personhood as such; resulting in a fourth relation to personhood. This is the most direct possibility, for it could also be; a flag, communal identity, a representation of the community, its underlying philosophy, and our interaction with it; resulting in fifth-relation. The sentiment only invokes a communal relationship and is not particularly individualistic as it sits above us like a scroll that is not readable but appears existentially safe. Only through an inquiry into an abstract representation of the communal identity can we read the scroll. We must relate to the relational theme in accordance with a yielding personal perspective and not reach a prudent perspective that cannot be applied to personhood.

Psychology as First-Relational

Psychology is the great theory of the contemporary era, which passages beyond philosophy and attempts to construct an investigation towards direct relational. The study of the 'superego' is done in direct relationship to personhood with selfhood presumably consisting of a 'superego'. The entire study is relational, with its substructure not requiring anybody to explain why one would be interested in such an inquiry. However, a sleight of hand occurs, since you can imagine in session for a lesson of psychology which could not be tolerate a direct relational experience throughout its duration. Rather we are creating a haven right above personhood which comprises the information but cannot be integrated in real-time since that would be an overload of information.

This haven of psychology, by its overwhelming notion of information, makes use of a theory of philosophy even as it appears to only be studying the individual in direct relation. That theory of philosophy is quite difficult to ascertain since it is unique for every student of psychology. One could entertain psychology to understand the self to further their social interaction, while another may do so to endow insight into the entirety of their experience. The latter is profound, carrying a great philosophy on its shoulders, and will be proven to further the boundaries of psychology. While the one who intends

---

[13] From this logicality, we may be able to understand the dichotomy of the familial locale being considered *1st place* and institution considered *2nd place*. (Oldenburg, Ray, *The Great Good Place*, 1989.)

to gain from psychology certain social advancement and a sense of relevance in the societal world will approach the psychological information as would a banker towards a profitable investment.

Abstraction and Monotheism

Abstraction as the Philosophy of Civilization

We find situations in which individuals that are assigned seclusion will cope with that neglected part of personhood, that of the communal aspects, by maintaining a rigorous interaction of abstract science, specifically mathematics.[14] While on the other end of the spectrum, there are people who have maintained their connection with the communal body by finding a quantity of nature or object that can serve as an effective surrogate to the known world of yesteryear. This can also be done through interpersonal relationships which would have each party represent the lost realm in proportion to each other and become a reservoir of the communal body. The method of abstraction, especially mathematics, is not to be overlooked since it emphasizes foundational elements to the structure of civilization.

As we have said, the basis for all civilization is its underlying philosophy, and with maintenance of that philosophy, even if the entire communal body withers away, it will prove self-sufficient. We are proposing that mathematics points to the primary philosophy, which supersedes specific civilizations and their itemized sub-thesis. If we were to find a person of any background who can maintain their communal connection through mathematics, then we can be sure that the subject is not culturally specific to a single civilization but constituting an overall theory of civilization.

What is within mathematics that merits such attention? And why is such

---

[14] Bond, Michael, *When People Are Isolated from Human Contact*, BBC Future, 2014. Hussain Al-Shahristani maintained his mental stability during a decade of solitary confinement by immersing himself in abstract thought, creating mathematical problems and attempting to solve them. Similarly, Edith Bone, a medical academic and translator, spent seven years in imprisonment, during which she constructed an abacus from stale bread and methodically cataloged her vocabulary across the six languages she spoke fluently.

material not pursued to produce an age of maturation or at least maintain any degradation of particular sub-civilizations? As we've elaborated henceforth, mathematics is numerical representations and their interactions with each other. Time and mathematics are closely related since they both rely on the division of a universal aspect or unifying matter. Without apportioning anything we could not create a mathematical formulation, and its first act is to divide or to envision a division in the unity of inquiry. Thus, mathematics is the theory of division which can further understand the unified whole and its parts.

Moreso, it also places recognition of the unified whole by its recognition of its parts. Analogous to a doctor who takes great care of the many parts of the body, while subsequently recognizing the body as a whole. In a certain sense, mathematics creates the availability for all disciplines by its call for both division and unified entities; a primal definition for *discipline*. One step further from all other disciplines is that the entire application of mathematics is a practical production of that theory; obliging the psyche to respect the unified entity through its subdivisions. Therefore, it is both consistent in an overarching theory of civilization and a practical implication that ensures its distribution throughout the psyche. The conceptual nature of civilization requires the interplay of unity and division. We can only entertain a conceptualization when we divide or separate components of personhood to allow for the construct of a psyche state to be relatable to personhood.

It is no wonder that Plato surmised the study of geometry, "as the knowledge which aims at the eternal, and not of aught perishing and transient."[15] We find his reluctance for geometry's pursuit in non-practical applications of daily life, with the axiomatic statement: "Something compels one to look at [the concept] *being* as appropriate; and at [the concept] *becoming* as inappropriate." This sentiment would demote the discipline of geometry as a concept of *becoming*, being in second-relation to personhood. If the study was the concept of *becoming*, implicating a further degree of relation by gaining an abstract conceptualization that does not directly link back to personhood, he was reluctant to deem it appropriate. Despite being of a further degree, there will always be a relation value, however overextended it might be from initial personhood.

The relationship to the abstract study of geometry would be to enter into its philosophy without acknowledging the process is being undertaken. There would be no reason to approach the geometric framework if there wasn't a universal system which has accordingly made itself relatable to the

---

[15] Plato, *Republic*, VII.

mainframe of higher-life-form. Despite the lack of articulated knowledge of that philosophy, the engagement with geometry is in context to that philosophy.

However, the study is in third-relation to personhood because there are two links in the direction of personhood. One is the link from abstract study to its underlying philosophy, two, the link between the philosophy and relatable aspects of personhood. As the study of geometry is usually performed under a collective body or institution, that develops to be part of additional sequential junctions. Consequently, a troubling scenario occurs when the relations are overextended to which we may not advance greatly by the end. The study itself would relate to the institution (1), which has the institution relating to oneself (2), all for the possibility of relating to a conception for that engagement (3) and finally the development of knowledge (4). This would eventually relate to the subcategory of knowledge, namely geometry (5), which relates to an underlying philosophy, one which relates to personhood (6-7). This example is under a sixth-degree relation, which in familial rapports is not even considered a domestic bond.

Hence, even with all these consequences, Plato argues: "That geometry is the knowledge that always is, not of something that comes to be and passes away and thus, can draw the soul toward truth and produce philosophical thought by directing upward what we now wrongly direct downward." Since geometry is bound to some sort of universal law, which permits it to have the benefit of not decaying through time or being corrupted as we have seen in contemporary disciplines, it becomes worthwhile even with the near possibility of an overextended relationship. Furthermore, the philosophy which accentuates geometry is so advanced and rudimentary for any sort of innovation that it becomes universal by its relevance to all personal affairs.

We could argue that psychology is eternal in its fundamental sense, however since it does not encompass the entire scope of existence or that of civilization, at least not at the scale which geometry embraces, it becomes available to more degeneration. The discipline of psychology depends on greater disciplines, which if corrupted during transmission would cause psychology in its many forms to become a pitiful weapon. Geometry has the defense of never falling prey to subsequent disciplines as it professes a structure of existence that can encompass much of the material and conceptual realm.

Theoretically, we can depart from our association to mathematics and thus its underlying philosophy, even as it has been proven to be universally factual. For it is only in the relationship of personhood to that dichotomy that it becomes a potent force for all other knowledge, and for the furthermost of civilization. The notion of 'universally correct' is only as good as the individuals who entertain that axiom, and without it, the notion of correct and incorrect are completely irrelevant.

Confirmation that Abstraction is the Philosophy of Civilization

We discover recorded individuals who can cope with great isolation for lengthy durations and find many with the attribute of observance to mathematics or other abstractions. This is because it encompasses within its substructure the blueprint of civilization and its potential developments. Accordingly, the entire city which was formerly known to the individual has now been internalized through the interaction with the underlying theory upon which the city rests. We could hypothesize that a rigorous interaction with mathematics would have a secluded individual successfully build an entire civilization without any subsequent interaction with the civilized world; granted that the memory remains intact.

This must be the case, because what other concept could explain the link between individual and communal body other than mathematical conceptualizations? What are the relics inherent within civilization and its corresponding cities which resolve the mass array of information that is naturally transmitted by interacting with the community? It couldn't be that $2 + 2 = 4$ comprises within it the cultural advancements of the civilized world. What can we identify in that equation that embodies the entire communal body? Even within the civilized world, we are dismayed at the immense amount of social reciprocity that is required to maintain that information, e.g., Institutions.

Mental Acuteness: The Attribute of Abstraction

We may want to attribute the ability for mental perseveration to be allocated to abstractions such as mathematics by supposing the upkeep of a sharp psyche. We underestimate the portions of personhood that are based on and influenced directly by the collective body. Without the collective body, even speech would be absent let alone advanced cognition. In connection to the case of feral man, Zingg writes, "All the cases of feral man agree with being mute, often despite an acute sense of hearing. Most cases made animal-like sounds when recovered. Also, among animal-reared children, there is but one case of recovery of speech beyond the degree of recovery recorded of the Wolf-child of Midnapore, Kamala, of the ability to say about fifty words. The failure of the development of speech, the most characteristic faculty of humanity, is of the greatest significance in the retardation of their mental faculties."[16] Had the effect of mathematics produced only a "sharpness of psyche," the feral man would have only lost the ability to speak by their lack of sharpness. With proper conditioning concerning a civilized structure, these feral individuals should have been able to regain that function. We can attribute this to some psyche adaptation, within the wild to have caused their speech abilities to be irreparably impaired.

Either we argue that mathematics comprises the entire development of cognition which allows for the progress of contemporary individuals, or we propose that mathematics is the theory of advanced cognition. As for the former, we can construct societies with perfection by having everybody study advanced mathematics as it contains all the advancements of cognition. Apparently, that is not the case because such a society wouldn't necessarily be deemed more advanced. We find that a mathematical society did not necessarily produce contemporary progression. Kline (1962) writes "Only a few ancient civilizations, Egypt, Babylonia, India, and China, possessed what may be called the rudiments of mathematics. The history of mathematics, and indeed the history of Western civilization, begins with what occurred in the civilizations of Egypt and Babylonia. Whereas that of China may be unnoticed because it was not extensive and had no influence on the subsequent development of mathematics."[17]

We are compelled to recognize that it is not the attribute of sharpness that is the method of actualization but rather the underlying theory that countenances the progression within the collective body. We may wish to contend, that rather than the astuteness of the psyche itself which is permitting one to remain connected to the collective body, the acuity awards the capacity towards memory traces of the collective body. These reminiscences can then be contemplated upon in a repetitive cycle. However, due to the duration in isolation, such a theory is improbable. One cannot rely on their memory to animate the present moment for an overextended duration.

We conclude that while mathematics produces sharpness of the psyche, it is not that attribute which ensures the psyche remains stabilized. A keen psyche could not further all the data necessary to produce an enhanced individual. Secondly, mathematics does not contain inherent information for notable counsel of the progressive world. Therefore, mathematics is the theory for civilization and followed appropriately, even during seclusion we

---

[16] Robert M. Zingg, *Feral Man and Extreme Cases of Isolation*, American Journal of Psychology, Vol. 53, No. 4.

[17] Morris Kline, *Mathematics: A Cultural Approach*, 1962, p.12.

will always be able to retain a civilized formula for interaction.

Center of the Individual

We take it for granted that the individual is assumed to be at the center of phenomena. Societies corresponding to ancient Egyptians did not take such an interpretation, for illustration, the ancient Theos *Seth* embodied the disordered aspects of the ordered realm. When an Egyptian or its system experiences disorderliness, they did not perceive that aspect according to individualistic experience or an inborn manifestation, but rather as an animation from a specific Theos. If they wished to have a more certain order, the course for correction wouldn't attempt differing personal choices. The approach would either have been to appease the Theos or to be contemptible towards it.

Even the concept of a "personal realm" would appear confusing to their psyche, as they did not have a notion of an internal subjective realm. Subjective and objective are strictly monotheistic derivatives, denoting a realm that is unified at the level of the individual, and another which is unified at the level of nature. This is why there is a lengthy ordeal for the distinction between subjective and objective, as we assume everything to be connected, begging the contemporary mind to ask, what is different about the individual and the external realm in which they occupy?

Ancient Theos represents the important concepts of individual experience. They did not have a Theos, for instance, a chair or a window, reserved for the essential concepts to be purely assumed to contain distinctive energy, resembling *fertility, death, mortality, wisdom, writing, love, motherhood, war, destruction, and healing*. The Theos *Ptah*, the Theos of craftsmen, would affect the craftsman's lifestyle.[18] A woodworker could not assume the craft and skill to be unique to their individualistic makeup since *Ptah* is perceived as the undeniable performer of the work. When the work fails, they do not assume an intrinsic failure. Learning the trade was assumed as the benevolence of the Theos, in part for allowing the craftsman to use the power of the Theos.

The individual serves as a conduit for the Theos to express itself. Instead of the center of attention positioned at the individualistic level, the center is concentrated on the metaphysical realm. People are viewed as deeply dependent on their Theos. At a certain point in their history, the Theos *Seth*

---

[18] Encyclopedia Britannica, *Ptah*, 2020.

came to be seen as an enemy who must be eliminated.[19] We could assume that people were seeking more order than the Theos was *providing*, with the only approach to confront the Theos of disorder. Because social beings were seen as conduits of the Theos' will, they did not entertain the notion of personal choice. Despite the principle that they were only conduits of the Theos' will, they still assumed they could influence the Theos and even eradicate them in a season of change. There lie the seedlings of monotheism as they begin to understand that they can control the Theos through appeasement and warfare. The fixation for controlling the Theos would be the preliminary stage for advancing life forms to seek and control phenomena itself, including the individual.

---

[19] "After the close of the New Kingdom, as Egypt lost its empire and later its independence, [disorder] and as the cult of Osiris grew in prominence, Seth was gradually ousted from the Egyptian pantheon. In the 1st millennium BCE his name and image were effaced from many monuments. He was now identified as a god of the eastern invaders of Egypt, including the Persians."
Encyclopedia Britannica, *Seth*, 2024.

Stages of Thought

The Use of Abstraction as a Methodology

The history of higher life form development is a subject that should be viewed from the vantage perspective of society's subjective encounter, encapsulating the individualistic nature of the queried people. We must acknowledge the magnitude of our progression and recognize that any comparison-based study requires a pre-conceived understanding of the disparity between ourselves and the subjects of historical inquiry. Without recognizing that gap of interpretation, we would be using devices of contemporary construction to understand a system which does not make use of such devices. The entire apparatus of engagement for these historical inquiries will be compelled into the domain of our system, providing us with more information about ourselves and less of the nature of our inquiry.

The contemporary individual differs from the ancient individual in terms of self-awareness and level of consciousness. Through the accumulation of collective knowledge, we had the opportunity to explore realms of existence that were previously unidentified. We must likewise identify the cognitive differences between contemporary and ancient societies, highlighting the realistic experience of our current state in contrast with them. The criticism against such a study is the skeptical nature of approaching a subject in this manner: one grants themselves the power to create a conceptualization alongside the study, essentially seizing the possibility of critiquing with any intervention of biases with the concluding research. By affirming that we must approach ancient history through the lens of 'them', we must first create a conceptualization that would be defined as 'them', to then produce our research. Undoubtedly, we can see the problem demonstrating itself; when we are allowed to define the people of inquiry while simultaneously inquiring into them.

This is coupled with the fact that we are comparing a brief span of history, a few thousand years, all within the backdrop of evolutionary biology, anthropology, and archaeology; all which do not scale at a low resolution. We would be creating a conceptualization of 'them' which does not inherently agree with these major disciplines and their developments. However, they all contain the susceptibility of approaching the subject from a contemporary conceptualization of science, which marginalizes the nuances of variation that can only be accessed, as would the subjective experience of the Egyptian. This I plead with you, is to allow me to define the Egyptian, while admittedly will not be accurate but will serve as a conceptualization that confiscates our contemporary bias.

Let us view the evolutionary progression as an approximation that transcends time, as the evolutionary timescale from primates to higher life form spans several million years. Furthermore, we should acknowledge that the progression did not occur in lateral increments but rather accelerated with time. The recorded history of higher-life-form represents a stretch of intense acceleration, for which a thousand years of the present era can equate to a million of prehistoric development.

Moreover, to capture this development, we could consider the ongoing mental developments accredited to societies. The rapid acceleration of higher-life-form primarily transpires in the psyche realm, as individuals harness the power of the psyche to surpass physical prowess. The evolutionary design is not unaware of these changes and, sure enough, can be seen as the chief arbitrator of these mental developments. Instead of expanding the organism, it has found a locality which if expanded, will reproduce itself at a speed rate which makes classic evolution seem uneventful. This is the psyche which can proceed with consciousness and rationality to produce an innovative notion at an incredible rate.

The psyche has reached a level of complexity which can be termed as an abstraction, which both produced self-awareness and social developments. Abstraction can be seen as the pinnacle of evolutionary focus, being of such importance for the ability of evolving itself. With this theme in mind, we can approach history as an emergent society that is becoming characteristically more abstract. Any moment of significant development in the post-history era can be recognized with a resultant upgrade or downgrade in the realm of abstraction. When we retroactively understand that abstraction is the cause of momentum within evolutionary cycles, we can input that notion into each era of inquiry to understand how this abstraction makes itself visible. Further, we gain the prerogative of reinterpreting ancient systems with a corresponding translation of abstraction.

Translating Abstraction

The ability to translate abstraction will arrive when we understand its consistency and by what method it developed over time. In addition, our innate self-awareness of the level of abstraction will offer a comparative view of each era of inquiry. The principles of these societies, in whatever they attend, are a part of our contemporary society and its thought progressions. Engaging them to be at a determinate level of abstraction, while we may practice a more complex version of it.

We cannot dismiss this, assuming that primordial aspects are somehow preceding contemporary society. This becomes the enigma of history, conceived as a preceding event, distinguished as an inquiry that diffuses the possibility for an examination of the condition of higher life forms. The form does not recreate itself, only comprehending a more complex lens to approach experience. History should be subject material that is accessed through a perception of the complexity in which each era approached personhood experience. In this way, it is both psychological and philosophical, serving the present era with relatable material. Every distinct activity for the historical period of ancient Egypt is part of the higher-life-form institute, one that we perpetually occupy is its abstract modification. All the occurrences of recorded history are currently a part of our culture and society, waiting to be elucidated according to a degree of abstraction.

Abstraction in History

When we examine the prioritization of *afterlife* during the Egyptian dynasties and we do so within a vacuum, it may appear far-reaching for contemporary subjectivity. With an analysis of how the Egyptians perceived life and death, it can offer comprehension into our subjective perspective. Their unique perspective on the afterlife led to an emphasis on the elaborate burial rituals. If we were to view them as we would ourselves, we may miss the realistic nature of their fixation upon the *afterlife*. Accordingly, we must find the contemporary equivalent of a finite degree of abstraction, one that correlates with their sympathetic attitude towards the afterlife.

We can posit many theories. First, they were persistent to preserve aspects, elements, or social beings that will endure for the maximum extended duration to contrast fading organic life. Second, they had an apprehension with the existential query of existence, a continuous inquiry throughout history. Third, having found animated life form to be a profound aspect, something that was introduced with stamina at that moment in history. This is something that is deeply influential for contemporary society, making it difficult to conceptualize a contemporary perspective that does not sanctify life form or a component of it.

From evolutionary history, we acknowledge that one of the establishing stages for higher life forms was the burial ritual. The Egyptians advanced this, especially in reference to the elaborate burial themes, which was a durable element in the sanctity of animation, in its woeful attempt at continuation. The idea of immortality was entertained by persons who valued life to a degree that there could be no justification for death. The contemporary individual will relate to all of these notions. We may approach the challenge of the higher-life-form value in a supplementary manner than the burial ritual, although the mere postulation for the sanctity, is one which we continue to interest. We may postulate that prioritizing the afterlife might be counterintuitive, distracting one from the sanctity of life. Still with the question of death simmering, other contemporary solutions will be entertained.

Similarly, just as we organized the concept of an afterlife, we must expand the study of ancient societies to include *individuality, life, death, Theos, meaning*, and other subjective views. What was it like to think in such a society? What was it like to communicate? To enter into their subjective experience, we must remove our newfound developments in each of these arenas. Thus, the question we may ask, how do we think and communicate to contrast the manner that these societies performed that very act? With this line of thinking, we incorporate the vast cognitive developments that contributed to each of their idiosyncrasies.

Types of Communication

We can start by examining how communication transpired during the ancient realm, facilitating cognitive development in ancient societies. Their communication can be divided into three categories, internal dialogue, the material linking two individuals, and communal relations. Internal dialogue is the basis of all communication, thereby making all social communication an exemplification of its content.

Communication can be provided through divergent methods; the primary being spoken and written language. The first known writing system was in use circa 3500 BC, and a full-fledged alphabetic writing system emerged in Greece circa 400 BC.[20] It is generally thought that the ancestry of the Greek alphabetic system could be traced to the Phoenician script, which might have been influenced by Egyptian, Aramaic, or Canaanite-Semitic writing. Alphabetic language and all written texts serve as technological advances for society, like the printing press or the digital innovation. The complexities that are present in the written form of communication suggest that individual interactions were consistently more intricate.

This leads us to the inquiry of the sequential progression of internal

---

[20] Aaron, P., & Joshi, R, *Written Language Is as Natural as Spoken language*, Reading Psychology, 2006.

language, although less overt to the researching platform since we do not comprise physical evidence of those developments. We must use different devices to gain a greater depiction that is accorded to the procession of internal language. This will assist our investigation of the procedure of the psyche, which, in turn, will endow intuition into their traditions and idiosyncrasies, determining the nature of our existing stature in reference to those idiosyncrasies, mending the disparity by identifying the cognitive modifications throughout history.

The premise is such, that the written forms of communication, in their exponential growth, had given ascendance to a parrelled internal formation of dialogue that was ruminating the psyche. The spoken form of communication is of less consequence, for it being an emulation of internal dialogue and not an intricate sophistication. In fact, we are asserting that the prominence of internal dialogue developed as a consequence of the written communication which extended its complexity, becoming internalized based on the written structure. This is the notion of abstraction, situated as the communication of the written forms which are then internalized, leading to a symbiotic relationship between the two; each providing a further realm of abstraction to be offered to the other.

Counterargument

Let us question our postulation that complex forms of communication correlate to complex inner dialogue. Kagan (1988) has found evidence that there is an association between complex thinking and the tendency to write in a relatively simple style. Suggesting that complex thinkers may have intuitively appreciated the value of simplicity in facilitating communication.[21] We can assert that poetry and its various forms of expression are characteristic of a cognitively developed person, even as they are simplistic practices of speech. We find that certain texts from ancient societies, such as the biblical corpus, valued simplicity, suggesting that complex thinkers were behind the texts. Concluding that, as social communication becomes simplistic it exemplifies a more complex internal dialogue.

However, let us challenge this traditional principle, in which quality is exemplary of a complex thinker. Using such forms may not demonstrate a complex thinker; rather, complex thinkers have the proficiency to recognize the quality of their own words. We may find that civilizations exclusively employed qualitative and simplistic forms of expression. This was the result of their inability to produce incoherent or low-quality speech. This ability, the

---

[21] Kagan, D., *Measurements of Divergent and Complex Thinking*, 1988.

trait of low-quality language, only appears when one is within the means to utilize their psyche beyond mere perception. Incoherent and poor-quality speech is more likely to arise from abstract and complex forms of thinking. We may venture to say that the ancient world did not have the ability of incoherent speech, just as animals do not retain that ability. There is a lack of supremacy in the mental apparatus, thereby not allowing abstract thought and its subsequent outcome; dysfunctional speech.

Abstract thought allows an individual to actively engage in one's internal dialogue alike when one speaks to a friend. The psyche becomes available to enter into itself and toil through the information as a communal body would have done. Without this approach to the psyche, it would mostly operate on autopilot and thoughts would not turn dysfunctional. Similar to breathing, an autonomous mode of the psyche, which if one were to consciously control, the ability for dysfunctional breathing presents itself. The natural mode of the psyche is not dysfunctional and rather serves to be as functional as possible. Only with the advent of supremacy over the psyche, otherwise termed abstract thinking, does the array of dysfunctional thoughts arrive. As a consequence, we have become accustomed to encountering low-quality texts in the contemporary era.

Even without all the progression for which we have obtained, the ancient realm was able to produce high-quality texts. For instance, the works of ancient Greek philosophers such as Plato and Aristotle, exemplify that ancient societies were capable of producing high-quality thought and expression. This may give the impression like a meta-critique on all contemporary culture and its path of progression; for a society to produce texts that contend with our own, a feat without all the advancements, determines them as a better society.

With our understanding of abstract thinking, they simply had no choice but to write with quality, individuals did not regulate the functionality of their psyches. As such, the psyche, in its natural state, is functional, producing quality speech and texts. This also features ancient societies who did not regularly contend with psychosis, to differentiate the contemporary era and its dealings. When psychosis did occur, it can be attributed to environmental elements and not a self-providing letdown. One must retain mastery over the psyche before having the ability to worsen the psyche into suboptimal states. Surely, nature can cause chemical and physical processes which obstruct the psyche in various ways, yet that would be limited to circumstance.

Codependency and Reduced Complexity

We are attempting to correlate complex communication with complex internal dialogue. Additionally, we can find a correlation between codependent dynamics and less complex internal dialogue. When a relationship becomes overly dependent, we can assume the thought material between them to be insignificant. For example, children are severely dependent on their parents, hence their relationship dynamic does not contain much separation. Therefore, we can acknowledge that the child's thoughts are not complex or abstract. Once the child develops, the psyche starts to internally make use of itself, creating a divide between itself and the external world. As abstract thinking becomes more abstract, so does the divide between one's relationships.

Moreover, we can convert the clause and find a correlation between the level of abstraction in social communication and the degree of abstraction in internal language. The progression from the Egyptian hieroglyphs to the Phoenician script marked a change in the level of complexity of communication. The abstraction in communication reflects the growing change within the psyche itself. Just as the complexity between individuals was pronounced, so was each individual in regard to themselves. They contained an array of pathways to mobilize their psyche, due to the growing complexity in the methods of social communication, revolutionizing internal language.

Alphabetic versus Hieroglyphics

Even if the spoken language is a manifestation of internal language, an individual would still need to conceptualize their internal language. We think in images and always require an image-to-text conversion, even with the alphabetic system. In our psyches, the letter 'A' is represented as a visual image, and we cannot conceive of the letter itself without this mental picture.[22] When we think of 'A', we are building a generative model representing visual knowledge derived from natural images. We then must imagine how a child thinks of the sound of 'A', which can be translated and understood from bodily motion, conveyed through sound visualizations in the shape of drawings.[23] However, this conceptualization can be limited, akin to trying to draw a piece of music, thus highlighting the inherent challenges and constraints in representing spoken language through visual means.

The Egyptians were basing their written communication on imagery, a less complex form of the alphabet. We can assume their internal language was lacking the nuance of alphabetical societies. Hieroglyphics, being image-

---

[22] Testolin, A., *Letter Perception emerges from Unsupervised Deep Learning*, Nature, 2017 — "We showed that learning visual symbols benefits from having part of the generative model representing domain-general visual knowledge derived from natural images."

[23] Frid, E, *Interactive Sonification of Spontaneous Movement of Children*, Frontiers in Neuroscience, 2016.

based, is less complex than the alphabet because letters can describe images with immense complexity, as we have seen in great works of literature. Images cannot describe other images with that same degree of nuance. For instance, a computer is text-based at its fundamental layer, which offers a degree of technological advancement. We would never consider building a computer that uses images as its foundational layer of communication.

The details of an image always matter more than the image itself, since the image contains endless possible interpretations, just as our experience in the manner we perceive has a bearing that is larger than the perception itself. We seek out what the image offers, and those offerings are the essential information of the image. Images, such as hieroglyphs don't contain the detailed information we are seeking from communication and conceptualization. Letters, words, and sentences are varied enough to offer intricate details for our perception.

Examples to Identify the Differentiation

Furthermore, another reason that the alphabet brings complexity is the fact that it is an abstraction. We don't want imagery as the method of communication because it would interfere with the nuance of information. For instance, if I want to communicate a rising tide, I may draw some large waves. Since the description of the tide is interconnected with the image, we will lose the complete portrayal of the rising tide by our personal connection to that proxy. If one deals in the trade of the sea, then the height of the pictorial waves may seem like a mediocre tide. While one who has never experienced the sea might assume the picture to portray a tsunami tidal wave. Thus, from an abstract point of view, the simple description of 'rising tide' is most clear, by the abstractive method of communication.

Let's take a concrete example from Egyptian hieroglyphs to demonstrate that abstract methods of communication are more precise than non-abstract. A *woman giving birth* would be a picture of a woman seated with a baby's head and arms coming out of her lower region.[24] This is an image to relate to another image, that of a woman giving birth, hence it is not abstract. The associations of this picture will become a barrier in effective communication, as one can assume it to be a difficult birth or an immediate one. Everyone's associations towards birthing will influence the final interpretation, with one assuming the picture to be a cephalic presentation, while another may view it as a seated position of birthing. The words 'woman giving birth' are abstract

---

[24] (George Douros, Public domain, via Wikimedia Commons)

enough that there is no other available meaning other than itself.

Written Language is an Expression of Internal Language

Additionally, after we have established the hierarchy of written language, the content which was written shall be a direct manifestation of internal language. Throughout all the discoveries of ancient Egypt, we have not produced any evidence which demonstrates that they conceptualized words as contemporary societies do so. They only possessed a library of mental imagery through perceptional data, and it was artistically expressed with hieroglyphics. Their thoughts could only have been in hieroglyphics or else an emulation of what they heard in the spoken language. Higher life forms will naturally express what is occurring in their psyches, their conceptualizations will be in the context of their written expressions. According to Aaron and Joshi (2006), written language is another manifestation of the natural endowment of the higher-life-form psyche and may not be treated as a proxy for speech. "The validity of the belief that spoken language represents the essence of the psyche, whereas written language is [only] a proxy for spoken language."[25] In terms of the hieroglyphics of ancient Egypt, the researchers determined that of an independent development of their writing from their spoken language. Written texts can now be used to determine the complexity of the author's thought processes.

Aaron and Joshi were bothered by the neglect of academia in using written language to study the psyche,

"Examples of linguists who have relied on spoken language to examine inner language are...These [various linguists] makes it apparent that spoken language is the window through which observations about inner language are made. In contrast, written language has been seldom exploited as a tool for exploring the nature of inner language because of the principle that it is an invention and an artifact."

Written and Internal Language

Let us further postulate that written language corresponds to internal language. We might not be able to create a distinctive separation between spoken language and internal language, as we may be bound to the same source. The forms of communication which are written are direct expressions to those that were initially thought. The nature of higher life forms is to

---

[25] Aaron, P., & Joshi, R, *Written Language Is as Natural as Spoken language*, Reading Psychology, 2006.

express their internal states, especially in their actions. Levin and Bus (2013) observe children who are unable to communicate meaning by writing eventually resort to drawing-like devices, indicating the primacy of drawing as a representational-communicative system.[26] To write would be extending their internal experience on paper. Moreover, if one contradicts their internal conceptualizations by drawing or writing against their psyche material, it will induce their internal state to align with their written expression. If one engages in nihilistic art, one will mechanically experience a nihilistic state.

Considering that images and mental conceptualizations influenced Egyptian written texts, it implies that their thoughts were rooted in images rather than words. Had it been in words, there would have been someone throughout its history to draw out and express the wordy images that were flowing through their psyches.

Conversely, they rather did retain a conceptualization of thoughts that did emulate the spoken language, similar to how children think. This emulation is an image-like production of sounds and emotional states in accordance with the sound. However, complex thinking was experienced through images, corresponding to hieroglyphics. The written language is the conceptualization of the highest degree of thought, and one who is illiterate will notwithstanding use a system of conceptualization to perform abstract thinking.

Emulation of Spoken Language Inhibits Abstract Thinking

One might argue that spoken language reflects the internal conceptualization of Egyptians, potentially enabling them to engage in abstract and critical thinking. We must remember that the Egyptian language contains sounds that have corresponding words and sentences. When we say that they contain words, we are employing our peculiar language to conceptualize history. They did not effectively contain words in themselves, as they were only able to pronounce the sounds they made while never being conceptualized as *words*.

We cannot perform abstract thinking by only using the emulation of spoken languages. For instance, take the example above, *a woman giving birth*. Pre-literate conceptualizations would be an image of a woman giving birth, as portrayed similar to the hieroglyphic image. Another conceptualization could be the emulation of the sound of the spoken words "woman giving birth." Consider using abstract thinking in this case, such as questioning the idea of the gender roles in the context of birthing. We would need to find an array of pre-heard sentences for this mode of thinking. The

---

[26] Levin, I., & Bus, A, *How is emergent writing based on drawing?* Developmental psychology, 2013.

sentence itself which provides the critical thought of gender roles must be emulated before the psyche could even bring forth an argument.

We may assume that emulation of language can bring about critical thinking as there is a memory bank of language at one's disposal. The basis of being critical of one's thoughts cannot be emulated from external sources. The usage of emulation demands that the entire language and its corresponding thoughts rest upon the simulation of a dialogue. The thoughts cannot exceed or develop beyond the experiences of external discourses. Even if the idea was discussed, thus leaving a trail of available internal discourses to analyze, to further the information with new angles would be outside the realm of possibility. Thus, the mere emulation of spoken language inhibits abstract thinking and would require an external conversation for any further rationality. Social discourse may be fruitless as well, since others may contain parallel information, creating a loop of information without a higher standard. This scenario does incrementally change, due to an elaborate and conscientious communal discourse, with diverse people and multiple classes contributing, eventually creating an output of critical thinking.

We can imagine it this way, upon a dialogue of only two people, despite the abstractive form which they are incapable of, there is still a form of differentiation between them. For instance, if one were to ask about a certain political occurrence, the other may return with the details that were heard. Yet the way in which it was said contains nuances that are different from the social material. This may be due to a misunderstanding or environmental influence, such as containing a preconceived notion towards the information owed to some personal situation in their life. Whatever the case, the relay of information will contain subtleties that are unknown to the social environment.

The recipient of the exchange must come to terms with those deviations, which normal sociality will unheed for being a deviation from recognized language and discourse. However, a partial component of its substance will be infused in the recipient's psyche, causing a form of disparity between the perfect understanding of language and this new material. This would require some meditation and would force the psyche to reproach itself based on the additional information. Thereby producing a slight form of rationality, even in the pre-abstract societies of the ancient world.

We may even attribute language itself to be a form of elementary abstraction, with the real psyche material unable to organically manifest through any communication medium. The information is completely embedded in the psyche and always requires a form of abstraction to produce a new communication device. Even animals will communicate with a communication device, exhibiting a slight form of abstraction between the experience of the information and the voiced version of it.

We may hypothesize that within the realm of animals, the degree of complexity of the communication device would be the level of abstraction they are utilizing. Higher life forms, on the other hand, may not always exhibit a complexity of language alongside a high level of abstraction. This is because there are communication devices other than language, such as social cues, facial expressions, and bodily gestures. These assist in creating a form of abstraction that can be complex even without the complexity of language. Furthermore, higher life forms can reach into abstraction without coinciding with language complexity. This can be done by containing a level of self-awareness that can grant access to abstraction without language.

This can be seen in its extreme manifestation for cases of schizophrenia, an individual residing in high levels of abstraction without the bearings of a similar level of complexity in language. However, in steady developments of intellectual strides, there would be a coinciding development of communication with that level of abstraction. We find that those who exist in high levels of abstraction retained a complex language form, such as philosophers. Mathematicians are to be considered engaging in secluded abstraction, which does not have abstraction for the entirety of mental experience.

Take a young child, when we ask them to attribute the gender of the birthing individual. Assuming that it is not a part of their mental library, they cannot build upon that theory without subsequent imagery. They must use a conceptualization device other than emulation to rationally think about the concept. The use of an image consisting of a female giving birth the assists the comparison of an image of a male not giving birth, deduces that females give birth. They can expand this thought process with the use of a fourth image that portrays a male in a stressed state prior the birth of a child, deducing that he may be involved more intimately than was speculated. This is the usage of hieroglyphics or imagery to critically think about something,

With progression, we developed imagery of language through the alphabet, which allowed critical and abstract thinking with unrestricted limits. Beck in his book, *Reading and Reasoning* states, "There is no reading without reasoning"[27], in which reasoning is developed based on literacy. Thus, Aloqaili (2012) reasserts that abstract thinking is correlated with literacy, after quoting various sources, "There is a well-established relationship

---

[27] I.L. Beck, *Reading and Reasoning*, 1989.

between reading comprehension and critical thinking"[28]

Counterargument – Communal Texts versus Individual Minds

This argument may be countered by the fact that the written accounts of ancient Egyptians were the dealings of communal aspects of life, possibly lacking direct correlation at the individual level. However, a group still demands expression from its constituents and their respective conceptualizations. Thus, we could take a government constitution and infer how the citizens orient themselves. The group is only an expression of its participating members and as the demographic shifts, so does the group's constitution. A society whose individuals conceptualize in words, would no doubt produce forms of expression that relate to that.

The Objective of Sociality in the Pre-abstraction Era

As the alphabet emerged, one gained the ability to communicate with themselves in a coherent manner. The social arena for the ancient realm was in service of helping each individual communicate with themselves. Each member did not encompass the tools to critically engage with internal dialogue and thus depended on society to develop their thoughts. Given that our social communication is based on many devices, not just that of language but, of action and modeling, social circles were the bedrock for personal introspection. The option to sit in solitude and develop one's thoughts was limited whilst being a part of a community offered a multitude of options.

One could model the leader's actions, and this would change a person's state and corresponding thoughts, comparable to the contemporary notion of exercise, which enacts alterations to thoughts and states. They intuitively could appreciate a certain person's behavior to model and incorporate all the persona and its intellectual content. We are using the notion of *thoughts* abundantly since we require a form of conceptualization to enjoin the process of thinking thoughts. However, we must agree that there are underlying thoughts that are pre-conceptualized, similar to how an animal "thinks."

Even in the relationship dynamic, one will receive many forms of communication that do not rely on the spoken word. This could manifest in the form of touch, mannerisms, facial expressions, and bodily movements, and will offer a vessel of thought-like information which can be mirrored.

The "introspection" of the prehistoric world would occur by the choice of social surroundings and the adherence to certain characters. Beyond mirroring and modeling, there would be no room for more insight to be

---

[28] Aloqaili, A, *The Relationship between Reading Comprehension and Critical thinking*, Journal of King Saud University, 2012.

gained. Societies did progress, although this progression came about through slight nuances and environmental factors. The nuances can come in the form of a "broken telephone" when the mirroring contrarily becomes adapted to what it was meant to be. The environmental changes such as famine, would be a pivotal event that would place tension on societies to develop in certain ways. Toynbee attributes a subsequent decline of civilization to a lack of adequate tension, as ironic as it sounds.[29]

We must view thought as an invention that strictly correlates with the advancements in social communication such as the alphabet, written texts, and complex vocabulary. When we contain twenty words for love, we also contain twenty ways to conceptualize the experience of love. The twenty initial states existed before; however, we didn't have the means to bring them into our conscious thoughts. With this realization, thought is not just an invention but rather continues to be invented through time.

Therefore, we could focus on any ancient civilization and view all its social and cultural particulars as compacted into the contemporary psyche itself. Their outlook on life is all the same as the contemporary realm, with the distinct differentiation being our internalization. With our psyche apparatus we can identify the specific things that correlate to the ancient realm's societal expression. For instance, the Egyptians, before they could engage in abstract thinking were attentive to assemblies of Theos'. We, as internalized higher life forms from the ancient world, don't need to engage in the Theos in its external form. Still, the Theos was an expression of an internal experience, being played out on the societal stage. Remember that ancient societies had great difficulty in engaging in internal dialogue and introspection, relying on the communion of the society and its members to hash out the insight that was contained within information. The Theos were the external form of an absolute individual experience, as such, we contain its lineage in our thought process.

Example of Abstract Translation - Mesopotamians

We will approach a couple of examples to further emphasize the practical implications of our argument. For instance, the Mesopotamians believed that water was everywhere, at the top, bottom, and sides, with the universe born from an enormous sea. We can contrast its contemporary manifestation as the formation of an embryo, surrounded by water, thus asserting that the individual is born from the universe. A further level of abstraction: the center of the individual encompasses the objective universe, and perhaps even more

---

[29] Toynbee, Arnold J, *A Study of History*, Vol III: The Growths of Civilizations, 1934.

abstract, perception is an internal design. Another more illustrative version: if nature is part of a single system, for which many higher life forms begin their development within water, it would be fair to place the entire universe as an embryo, surrounded by water. A dynamic version: water is the most essential element for life and is deserving of its dependence.

Another example for a more idiosyncratic interpretation is the common Mesopotamian principle that a Theos has the ability to indicate future events through omens; which could be interpreted through astronomy and astrology. Since omens via the planets were produced without any higher-life-form action, cosmic in orientation, they were seen as most powerful. Contrary to that, they also believed that the events which these omens foretold were also preventable.

The notion that a Theos could communicate through mediums such as omens, is the same notion as depicting the supreme level of individual experience can produce notions which can be interpreted by normative experience. The application of the omens upon planetary bodies produces a more realistic relation to our perception, being relatively visible and overhead, metaphorically and physically. This is why we cannot dispel the primordial version of heavens from contemporary discourse. Even with every scientific notation to the contrary, upon waking to this hovering entity, we still attribute and relate the experience as such.

Heaven is related to the psychological traits in which they are overarching selfhood, established by the superego, imagination, and intuitions. We could assert to only approach reality from abstract study and its realizations, however, we still require relatable entities that serve to expand our own experience of personhood. We could imagine that one who is withheld from the experience of 'heaven' corresponds to a loss of their grasp of the grandiosity of their psyche. An abstraction will never replace the realized experience, which so happens to be dependent upon it.

This Mesopotamian principle indicates the commencement of internalizing the notion of an external Theos to appropriate individual experience, creating an entire discipline of astrology which seemed irrefutable as a part of nature. Once the Theos is grounded in the scientific realm, it can be studied with objectivity, creating a better understanding of the Theos but also of nature and subjectivity. This Theos is a representation of our subjective mode during its superior state, with the omens being the insightful intuitions that demand a form of rationality to be extrapolated. In this context, intuition is the omen, while the discipline of astrology is the process of rationality to that poetic intuition. The thesis of a categorical Theos would be that these intuitive measures are incorporated under a single entity called personhood and individuality.

Anthropomorphization

There is a cultural agreement that the Theos must modify alongside the populace to retain its superior position, but not in the sense of anthropomorphizing the entity; which would smear a projected higher-life-form version upon the Theos to segregate the Theos' power. Anthropomorphization would be contrary to diagnosing the abstract version of the ancient idea of Theos. Anthropomorphization, elaborate in Greek mythology, is the beginning stage of an abstract form of atheism. This has the Theos become a character for an art exhibition, which can be interacted or disremembered without consequence. This could have been done, as may be argued, to internalize rationality and detach from the archaic form of an animated Theos. However, with the approach towards such projection, it would rather dispel the Theos from dynamic interaction.

The contemporary form of anthropomorphization would be utilizing grand intuitions, superego sentiments, as well as premonitions and poetic sentiments, and casting them as metaphorical art installations of the psyche which have no bearing on actual personhood. It is no wonder that the prolific Greek intellectuals have missed the sensational and emotional realms of the higher-life-form condition, waiting for consorts such as Shakespeare to produce poetry and theater for the universal objective. This had manifested in their social environment with the downcast of femininity and womanhood, to be attributed nearer to slavery than to manhood.[30]

Scholars are quick to downplay our qualms about the seeming contradiction of intellectual expansion that coincides the feminine disregard by cataloguing those Greeks as olden. The management of femininity was conscious and specific; an intricate part of their thought and philosophy. When approaching rationality as the only form of respect, one would be downplaying the Theos as a theater performance, the ensuing neglect of the realm of nuanced and personal intuitions and emotions.

Example of Abstract Translation - Imperialization

A final example is the concept of conquest and imperialization of the ancient world. This was an evolved phenomenon that is not always a part of the contemporary realm. Part of its clause is a superior figure dominating over the landmass to partake and interact with the subjects. The contemporary version of this, which is more evident than the others, is controlling a system.

---

[30] Aristotle, *Politics*. Section One.

This is to exercise control over oneself and participate in every aspect that comes into purview, which is to interact in an influential manner with all the components. This influence varies upon the intended thesis of the arbitrator of control, for control does not dictate what the reason for the adamant influence. This is found to be missing from Foucault's perspective of power or control, in that there is no distinction as to the aim of the controller, rather they are coupled into one label of inquiry of power.

We can never imagine a scenario in which one seeks to influence another without a certain aim other than the influence. If it were for the mere sake of influence, we must dig deeper and ask what the underlying reason is. We eventually encounter an objective to not lose the preceding access to those components of progress. This can be further inquired to find that the preceding points of access provide certain benefits and amenities to the arbitrator of control, so that the aim is one of pleasure and benefit from them. Which if we were to be philosophical, is to provide the host of power with the ability to grant pleasure to the arbitrator of control.[31]

When a country sets its sights on a new territory, it seeks to expand itself. When an individual identifies new aspects of themselves, they are also embarking on an expansion. To expand is to develop, and if that clause is to remain a part of our contemporary lens, then it will manifest externally. However, the notion of expansion can contain many interpretations; with one existing for the betterment of subjective experience, to provide insight for the confused states of the psyche, to find heightened pleasure from the experience, to perpetuate one's existence upon the communal landscape, to enlighten the psyche components which seem to be lacking substance, to become more self-sufficient within the mental apparatus.

---

[31] Foucault, Michel. *Discipline and Punish*, 1977.

www.ingramcontent.com/pod-product-compliance
Lightning Source LLC
Chambersburg PA
CBHW070119030426
42335CB00016B/2207